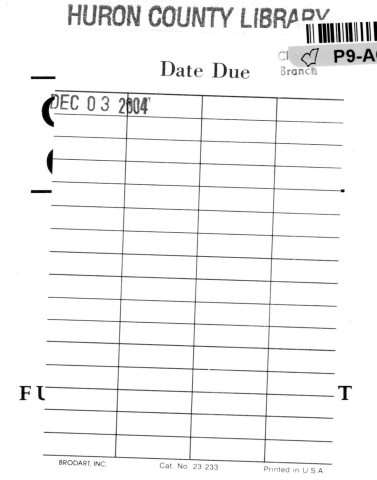

F U   T

D. Paul Schafer

WORLD CULTURE PROJECT

ISBN: 1-895661-00-5   (Set)
ISBN: 1-895661-06-4   (Volume 6)

TABLE OF CONTENTS

THE CONCEPT OF CANADIAN CULTURE

> We commonly use the term "culture" to describe professional artistic or intellectual activity — books, theatre, movies, television, art, music, ideas.
>
> But that's only the narrowest of definitions.
>
> Canadian culture is all these things, but it is much more....
>
> It's the sum of our particular experience and interests as a community, the blending and refining of a set of values, traditions and activities that define us as a nation.
>
> Max Wyman[1]

What is Canadian culture? This is a question that has confronted and confounded Canadians for generations.

For many Canadians, the problem is not worth worrying about. Either it will solve itself in the fullness of time, or there are too many different concepts and definitions of Canadian culture from which to choose.[2] In either case, having spent little time and energy wrestling with this complex problem in the past, many Canadians are inclined to assume there is little point spending a lot of time and energy on it in the future.

There are many reasons why this traditional response to the problem of determining what is Canadian culture is no longer advisable. The dangers and consequences are just too great.

In the first place, the problem will not go away. It will fester in the side of Canada and Canadians until it is set right.

---

[1] Max Wyman. "Canadian culture is all we've got — let's protect it." *The Weekend Sun.* Saturday, March 18, 1995. Vancouver. 1995. p. D3

[2] D. Paul Schafer. *The Character of Canadian Culture.* World Culture Project. Scarborough. 1990. p. 2-43.

In the second place, there is an enormous amount of confusion over the nature and meaning of Canadian culture.[3] For some Canadians, Canadian culture is the arts. For others, it is the legacy from the past or the "cultural industries." And for still others, it is leisure-time activity, shared values and beliefs, a way of life, a state of mind or a means of interacting with the natural environment. Little wonder it is the subject of so much confusion and controversy.[4]

In the third place, it makes Canada and Canadians vulnerable to countries which do have a strong understanding of their culture and the reasons for identifying, developing, understanding, promoting, protecting and exporting it. As the history of imperialism and colonialism demonstrates only too well, countries which fail to take the time and trouble to wrestle with the nature and meaning of their culture immediately run the risk of having their culture and entire way of life dominated by others.

In the fourth place, it perpetuates the problem of Canadian identity. Canadians can hardly expect to solve their identity crisis if they don't have a good understanding and awareness of their culture and the reasons for developing, promoting and appreciating it.

In the fifth place, it exacerbates the tensions, divisions and conflicts which exist throughout the country over the nature and meaning of the country's culture, particularly among French Canadians, English Canadians, the native peoples and other groups of Canadians who have vastly different views with respect to what culture is, what it means to themselves and others, and how important it is in the total scheme of things.[5]

---

[3] This problem is not unique to Canada and Canadians. It is a problem for many countries in the world and is part of the larger problem of defining culture in general. See Alfred Kroeber and Clyde Kluckhohn. *Culture: A Critical Review of Concepts and Definitions.* Vintage Books. New York. 1952.

[4] D. Paul Schafer. *The Character of Canadian Culture.* op. cit. p. 2-43.

[5] In general, English Canadians tend to perceive culture more narrowly than French Canadians, native peoples and minority groups. Conflict between these groups is inevitable because there are markedly different views about the importance and relevance of culture.

In the sixth place, it increases the possibility that important aspects of the country's heritage will be lost, neglected, ignored, eroded or traded away because they are not recognized as fundamental parts of Canadian culture in the first place. For example, every day significant aspects of Canada's agricultural, industrial and architectural heritage are lost or eroded because they are not regarded as vital aspects of Canadian culture. And what is true for Canada's agricultural, industrial and architectural heritage is equally true for Canada's natural and environmental heritage. Significant parts of this heritage have been left unprotected in the free trade agreements or bargained away because they are not really deemed to be integral parts of Canadian culture in the first place. And this despite the fact that many Canadians would contend that the relationship Canadians have with "the land" and the natural environment speaks more directly to Canadian culture than anything else.

Finally, and perhaps most importantly, failure to ascertain what is meant by Canadian culture means that Canada may fail to live up to its full potential. Not only will the resources of the country be less developed than they might otherwise be, but also the country will not be able to make its full contribution to international development and world progress because it does not have a good understanding of its culture and the reasons for developing and promoting it.

If these dangers and consequences are to be averted in the future, it will be essential for Canadians to find a viable solution to this problem. Failure to do so will exacerbate even more the basic issues and tensions which are playing havoc with the country and its citizenry.

THE OFFICIAL CONCEPT OF CANADIAN CULTURE

The simplest and most straightforward solution to the problem of determining "what is Canadian culture" would be for Canadians to adopt the "official concept of Canadian culture" as their overall concept of their culture. This would make it possible for all Canadians to share a similar reality and common understanding about the nature and meaning of their culture.

While many Canadians may find it difficult to accept, there is an official concept of Canadian culture slowly but surely working its way into the public domain and the collective consciousness. It is a concept which equates the country's culture with "the arts, heritage and cultural industries."

While there may be a great deal of debate and disagreement about how the component parts of this concept should be perceived and defined,[6] this is more or less what is meant by "Canadian culture" when the term is used in political, governmental and corporate circles,[7] reported on in the media, talked about at national and international conferences, written about in official publications, dealt with for purposes of free trade agreements, and promoted abroad.[8]

Identification of the "official concept of Canadian culture" is necessary in order to differentiate it from other concepts of Canadian culture, such as concepts utilized by scholars, educators, academic institutions, professional associations, special interest groups and citizens at large. Thus, while individual Canadians and specific interest groups may prefer to define Canadian culture more broadly or more narrowly — as the arts taken by themselves, multiculturalism, recreational activity, values, traditions and beliefs, a way of life, a state of mind, or a dynamic and organic whole — in an official, public sense,

---

[6] The arts are generally deemed to include music, theatre, dance, mime, painting, sculpture, writing, prose and poetry. Heritage is generally deemed to include art galleries and museums, and the cultural industries are generally deemed to include publishing, radio, television, film, video, sound recording, commercial theatre and the like. There has always been a considerable amount of debate with respect to whether the crafts, architecture, town planning, libraries, archives, sports and multiculturalism should be included in these definitions, as well as whether these definitions should include "popular" as well as "classical" activity.

[7] See for example, the Task Force on Professional Training for the Cultural Sector in Canada. *Art is Never a Given.* Ministry of Supply and Services Canada. Ottawa. 1991. pp. 111-112. Also see, Research and Evaluation Section. The Canada Council. *Artstats: Selected Statistics on the Arts and Culture in Canada.* 1st edition. The Canada Council. Ottawa. 1993. (See Section One on: Estimated Size of the Cultural Sector).

[8] William Littler. "Budapest to Get a Taste of Canadian Culture." *Toronto Star.* February 1991. p. B5.

Canadian culture is almost always equated with the arts, heritage and the cultural industries.

Acceptance of the official concept of Canadian culture as the country's overall concept of its culture is very tempting. For a country that has been pressed both internally and externally for decades to come to grips with the nature and meaning of its culture, here is a tailor-made solution. Not only is the official concept of Canadian culture rapidly winning converts and gaining currency throughout the country, but also adoption of it would make it possible for all Canadians to share a general agreement and common sense of understanding about the nature and meaning of their culture.

Sharing a general agreement and common sense of understanding on Canadian culture would not be the only benefit to be derived from adoption of the official concept of Canadian culture as the country's overall concept of its culture. A number of other benefits would be experienced as well.

By conceiving and defining Canadian culture as the arts, heritage and the cultural industries, the official concept focuses on tangible objects, artefacts and activities like plays, concerts, paintings, books, records, films, tapes and the like which can be bought, sold, touched, handled, exchanged, experienced, traded and talked about. This has the advantage of confining Canadian culture to physical and material items, thereby side-stepping the thorny problem of having to confront a whole host of deep and profound conceptual, theoretical, philosophical and practical problems.

It also makes it possible to concentrate on the development of a "cultural sector" which is very well defined and specific. It is a cultural sector composed of countless individuals, institutions, facilities and activities in the performing, exhibiting, creative and literary arts, film, broadcasting, publishing and sound recording which brings a great deal of fulfilment and happiness to millions of Canadians each year.[9]

9 Department of Communications. *Arts Consumer Profile*. Department of Communications. Ottawa. 1991.

However tempting it is to adopt the official concept as the country's overall concept of its culture, such a temptation must be resisted for several very specific and significant reasons. For despite the fact that it resolves a number of problems related to the search for an acceptable definition and understanding of Canadian culture, it creates far more problems than it solves.

In the first place, it marginalizes and trivializes Canadian culture by defining the country's culture in such narrow terms that it is given an extremely low priority in the total scheme of things. Secondly, it represents a politically-expedient solution to what is essentially a deep and profound philosophical, conceptual and practical problem. Thirdly, it makes Canada and Canadians dependent on cultural concepts, definitions, values, attitudes and practices prevalent in other countries, most notably European countries and the United States. Finally, and perhaps most importantly, it excludes many activities that a significant number of Canadians would consider to be the very essence of their culture. A moment spent reflecting on each of these problems is richly rewarding because it helps to put the official concept of Canadian culture in proper perspective and open the doors to an alternative way of looking at and defining Canadian culture.

In a country where money acts as a measure of value as well as a medium of exchange, defining Canadian culture very narrowly as the arts, heritage and cultural industries marginalizes and trivializes Canadian culture because it leads to the conclusion that the country's culture is not really all that important in the total scheme of things because very little money is spent on it. Clearly, if it was important, governments, corporations, foundations and Canadians generally would be spending a much larger portion of their budgets on it.

One consequence of this is that there are never sufficient funds to address some of Canada's most deep-seated problems, such as the problem of cultural identity, cultural sovereignty, and relations between the French, the English, the native peoples and other groups of Canadians. While much lip service is paid to these problems and the need to find viable solutions to them, in actual fact they are allowed to fester in the side of Canada and Canadians generation after generation because there is neither the political will, public commitment or financial resources to deal with them.

Clearly these problems will persist as long as governments, corporations, foundations and Canadians generally adhere to the official concept of Canadian culture. The reason for this is not difficult to detect. The official concept of Canadian culture is essentially a political solution to what is in effect a deep-seated and fundamental conceptual and practical problem. It is the problem of how to "operationalize" culture and deal with it in governmental, corporate, foundation and public and private affairs. What better way to do this than to conceptualize and define culture very narrowly and control it within strict limits?

When Canadian governments set up "cultural departments and agencies" in the late fifties, sixties and seventies, they were immediately confronted with the thorny problem of having to come up with an operational definition of culture and Canadian culture for administrative, planning, policy and funding purposes. How was the work of cultural departments and agencies to be differentiated from the work and activities of other government departments and agencies? Who was to receive "cultural funding" and for what purposes? Rather than wrestle with the problem of working out an understanding of culture in general and Canadian culture in particular which meshed with reality, it was infinitely easier to cast an eye around the world for a tailor-made solution to the problem.

The experience of European countries proved very enticing and timely in this regard. Not only were most European governments defining culture in narrow and restrictive terms as the arts and heritage, but also European countries provided excellent models of how culture could be controlled, contained and dealt with in government.

The creation of the Canada Council is very revealing and informative in this respect. When the Council was established in 1957 following a recommendation in the Massey-Lévesque report of 1951, it was modelled along the lines of the Arts Council of Great Britain[10] and placed at arm's length from the political process.[11] Not only was the cultural part of the Canada Council's mandate defined in terms of the arts and heritage, but also the Council had to wait many years before it received any appropriations from public funds. This is because it depended in the early years on the interest from an endowment which was established by the federal government following the death of two wealthy benefactors.

While the arts and heritage component of the official concept of Canadian culture can be traced to Great Britain, the Arts Council of Great Britain and concepts of culture prevalent in Europe, the cultural industries component can be traced to the United States and the shift that is taking place in many parts of the world from a "European concept of culture" to an "American concept of culture." While the roots of Canada's encounter with the cultural industries in this sense can be traced to the early part of the twentieth century and the establishment of "cultural agencies" like the Canadian Broadcasting Corporation and the National Film Board, the real reason for the inclusion of the cultural industries in the official concept of Canadian culture has much more to do with the rapid growth of the cultural and communications industries in the modern world and the key role the United States is playing in this. Whereas the European concept of culture focuses largely on the arts and heritage, the American concept of culture focuses squarely on the cultural industries of publishing, radio, television, film, video, sound recording and communications.

---

[10] While the Arts Council of Great Britain was created to deal exclusively with the arts and heritage, the Canada Council was created to deal with the social sciences and humanities as well as the arts and heritage. The reason for this had a great deal to do with the mandate of the Massey-Lévesque Commission, which was established in 1949 to examine the plight of higher education as well as the arts, heritage, sciences, and humanities in Canada. When the Canada Council was created in 1957, it included responsibility for both the social sciences and humanities as well as the arts and heritage. The jurisdictional and administrative difficulties resulting from this hybrid solution are apparent when the histories of the Canada Council and the Social Sciences and Humanities Research Council are juxtaposed and compared.

[11] The arm's length principle is firmly established in Canada and is applauded by both the arts community and the political community for its protection of artistic freedom and separation of the arts from the political process. Nevertheless, it is not without its shortcomings. By distancing the arts and culture from governments and the political process, it has profound financial and budgetary implications. The recent financial constraints and cut-backs imposed on the Canada Council and the country's cultural agencies serve to confirm this.

Here again, political expediency rather than commitment to coming to grips with the real nature and meaning of Canadian culture serves to explain why the cultural industries have been added to the official concept of Canadian culture. Not only does it speak volumes about the impact of American perceptions and concepts of culture on Canada — perceptions and concepts which are much more market-oriented and profit-driven — but also it speaks volumes about the need to protect Canada and Canadians from the steady encroachment of American media products and cultural industries in Canada.[12]

As a result of historical and contemporary developments like those in Europe and the United States, most of Canada's government cultural departments and agencies now view the arts, heritage and the cultural industries as the key components in their mandates.[13] While there may be some variations on this pattern depending on the needs and interests of particular departments and agencies, especially in such areas as sports, tourism, recreation, multiculturalism and citizenship, the large majority of the country's government cultural departments and agencies now define culture in general and Canadian culture in particular in terms of the arts, heritage and cultural industries. It is a way of thinking about and dealing with Canadian culture that has been strongly influenced and reinforced in recent years by the signing of the free trade agreements. Protection of "Canadian culture" for purposes of these agreements means protection of Canada's arts, heritage and cultural industries.

It is clear from this brief examination of the official concept of Canadian culture that it is an imported rather than indigenous concept.[14] Not only is it a hybrid of the American and European concepts of culture,

---

12 Department of Communications. *Vital Links: Canadian Cultural Industries.* Ministry of Supply and Services Canada. Ottawa. 1987.

13 See the Canadian Conference of the Arts' *Directory* of governmental departments and agencies for confirmation of this.

14 Canada is not the only country in the world to define its culture officially in imported rather than indigenous terms. Many countries in the world define their culture in these terms. See, for example UNESCO's *Studies and Documents on Cultural Policies for Member States.* Also see, Pekka Gronow. "The Definition of the Sphere of Cultural Development." in *Planning for Cultural Development: Methods and Objectives.* Document of the Expert Meeting at Hanasaari, Espoo, Finland. March 17-19, 1976. Cultural Development Dossier 9-10. UNESCO. Paris. 1976.

but also it tends to make Canada and Canadians dependent on cultural concepts, definitions, practices, policies, perceptions and values prevalent in Europe and the United States.

While this dependency has many advantages, particularly in terms of the emphasis it places on excellence, creativity, appreciation of a priceless legacy of artistic works and access to a large and distinctive array of historical and contemporary resources and opportunities, it also comes at a very steep price. For as Canadians and people in other parts of the world are increasingly discovering to their consternation, the price is a heavy reliance on European and especially American cultural programming, adoption and aping of American and European cultural concepts and values, loss of autonomy, identity and sovereignty, utilization of culture as an instrument of economic policy, emphasis on privatization and the marketplace, and a considerable downsizing in the public sector's commitment to culture.

No sooner is the official concept of Canadian culture exposed as an imported rather than indigenous concept than the main reason for rejecting it is revealed. For while it possesses many benefits and has certain advantages, it fails to come to grips with the real nature and meaning of Canadian culture. This is because it excludes many activities that a significant number of Canadians would deem to constitute the very essence of their culture.

Most conspicuous among these activities are sports like hockey, figure-skating, basketball and lacrosse, recreational pursuits like canoeing and snow-mobiling, social programmes like health care and day care, transportation and communications endeavours like railroads and long-distance satellites, economic practices like mining and the extraction industries and environmental activities like love of nature and landscape. Since many Canadians feel these activities epitomize Canadian culture better than anything else, to contend that Canadian culture can be conceived and defined without reference to these and other fundamental aspects of the country's cultural life is not only misleading, it also represents a serious distortion of Canadian culture. Not only does it mean that many of the most serious problems confronting Canada and Canadians never get addressed properly — problems which are deeply etched in the Canadian psyche and are constantly threatening to undermine the country and rip the country apart — but also it means that Canadians are being deprived of an opportunity to really get to know and understand their culture.

Recognition of this fact should cause Canadians to reject the official concept of Canadian culture as the solution to the problem of determining what is Canadian culture. On the one hand, it fails to come to grips with the breadth, depth, complexity and reality of the country's culture. On the other hand, it is far too dangerous to carry forward into the future. In fact, the longer the practice is continued, the more dangerous the consequences will be.

Rejection of the official concept of Canadian culture immediately opens the door to alternative concepts of the country's culture. Naturally there are many views and opinions about what this concept should be. Clearly it should be a concept which is consistent with the Canadian situation and the experiences of Canadians rather than with the experiences of other countries and other peoples. In order to do this, it should spring naturally and organically from the roots, soil and traditions of Canada and Canadians, rather than being artificially grafted on to the country from the outside or superficially imposed on the citizenry for reasons of political expediency and bureaucratic convenience. For only in this way will it reflect Canada's true cultural nature, as well as provide an understanding and definition of Canadian culture which is consistent with the reality of the Canadian experience.

A HOLISTIC CONCEPT OF CANADIAN CULTURE

The key to coming to grips with this much more indigenous and authentic way of looking at and dealing with Canadian culture lies in the realization that Canadians have come together in association over the centuries for the express purpose of living together in the world and working out their association with the world. In the process of doing this, they have created a culture which shares certain similarities with other cultures but in the end is distinctive and unique.

In order to create and sustain this culture, it has been necessary for Canadians to address a whole host of difficult and demanding cultural challenges. How is the world visualized and interpreted? How is survival guaranteed? How is the need for food, clothing, shelter, health, welfare, jobs, income, education, spiritual renewal and aesthetic expression dealt with? How are environmental, economic, political, social, educational and religious systems planned and developed? How are communities, regions and the country as a whole organized? How is geographical space occupied? How is the quality of life improved? And how are relations conducted with other peoples, other cultures and the world at large? In other words, how is a culture created which meets the needs, concerns, and requirements of Canadians for survival, security, fulfilment and well-being?

It is clear from these questions that Canadian culture is concerned with much more than the arts, heritage and cultural industries. While the arts, heritage and the cultural industries are exceedingly important because of their communicative value and expressive ability, Canadian culture is concerned with the whole way Canadians perceive the world and act in the world.

Taking a cue from this, it is possible to define Canadian culture as "the way Canadians visualize and interpret the world, organize themselves, conduct their affairs, elevate and embellish life, and position themselves in the world.[15] Each component of this "holistic concept of Canadian culture" contributes a great deal to the understanding of the nature, meaning, subject matter, importance and complexity of the country's culture.

---

[15] D. Paul Schafer. *The Cosmological Concept of Culture: Canadian Culture Used as a Case Study for Illustrative Purposes.* World Culture Project. Markham. 1992.

How Canadians visualize and interpret the world deals with all the cosmological, philosophical, theological, mythological, scientific, aesthetic and ideological beliefs, principles and convictions which Canadians possess. These beliefs, principles and convictions constitute the cornerstone of Canadian culture because how Canadians visualize and interpret the world determines in large measure how they act in the world. As such, they deserve the greatest priority and utmost attention because they relate so fundamentally to what Canada and Canadians are all about and how Canadians relate to themselves, each other, other species, other countries, other cultures and the world at large.

How Canadians organize themselves deals with all the decisions Canadians make with respect to the development of economic systems, political processes, social structures, technological practices, communications networks, electronic highways and the development of towns, cities, regions and the country as a whole. Whether the country is organized as "a community of communities," "a nation of nations," or "a federation of provinces, territories and regions" — as well as whether the country is organized along liberal, conservative, socialist or capitalist lines — are all matters which fall within the scope of how Canadians organize themselves in space and time.

How Canadians conduct their affairs deals with the character of Canadians' lives, and with it, decisions about consumer practices and consumption expenditures, business investment, education, living arrangements, family life and the like. A great deal of factual information already exists on this particular aspect of Canadian culture as a result of census data, statistical studies, opinion polls, consumer surveys and a variety of activities undertaken by specialized institutes and professional associations.

How Canadians elevate and embellish life deals with all the decisions Canadians make with respect to artistic, social and spiritual life, ethical and religious practices, recreational and leisure-time activities, intellectual pursuits, and moral and ethical development. Many of these decisions are instrumental in making life a fuller, richer, healthier and more fulfilling affair that it would otherwise be.

And how Canadians position themselves in the world deals with all the decisions Canadians make with respect to relations with other countries, cultures and peoples, as well as their overall diplomatic posture and geopolitical position in the world. Included here are a complex series of activities and issues related to the negotiation and signing of trade agreements, foreign affairs, developmental assistance, diplomatic arrangements with other countries and areas of the world such as the United States, Europe, Africa, Asia, Latin America, the Commonwealth and la Francophonie, and peace-keeping initiatives. When Northrop Frye said the most important question confronting Canadians is not "Who are we?" but "Where is here?", he was focusing attention on the crucial importance of place and Canada's overall geographical location and geopolitical positioning in the world.

When Canadian culture is perceived and defined in this all-encompassing, holistic way, it is obvious that the scope and subject matter of Canadian culture is enormous. Not only is Canadian culture concerned with all aspects and dimensions of life in Canada — from the theoretical and the conceptual to the practical and specific — but also it is concerned with Canada, Canadians and Canadian society as a whole.

Are there grounds for conceptualizing and defining Canadian culture in such comprehensive and holistic terms? Indeed there are. When Canadians talk about being "the products of their culture," they tend to mean they are the products of much more than art forms, heritage activities and cultural industries. More generally, they tend to mean they are products of political, economic and educational systems, recreational activities, social norms and mores, religious values and attitudes, and environmental policies and practices as well as art forms, heritage activities and cultural industries. In other words, they are the products of everything that exists in their culture or their culture **as a whole**.

It is not only individual Canadians who talk about and visualize their culture in this way. Canadian politicians also talk about and visualize Canadian culture in these terms. When Flora MacDonald was Minister of Communications, she had this to say about Canadian culture:

> "Culture" is a concept with many different meanings. It certainly refers to artistic and literary activity. But it also has sociological and anthropological connotations — bringing to mind the ways in which societies and groups communicate and, indeed, define themselves.
>
> Canadian culture encompasses all these things. Ultimately, it is the substance and reflection of who we are and what we form as a people. Our landscape is part of it; our tastes, our languages, our pastimes, the way we view the world, these all enter in.[16]

Flora MacDonald is not the only political official to endorse this much more holistic way of looking at culture in general and Canadian culture in particular. Canada, along with the other member states of UNESCO, was a signatory to the following definition of culture which was adopted at the Second World Conference on Cultural Policies (Mondiacult) in Mexico City in 1982:

> Culture ought to be considered today the whole collection of distinctive traits, spiritual and material, intellectual and affective, which characterize a society or social group. It comprises, besides arts and letters, modes of life, human rights, value systems, traditions and beliefs.[17]

The arguments for adopting this much more comprehensive view of culture were set out even more forcefully in the planning documents and working papers for the World Decade for Cultural Development:

---

[16] Department of Communications. *Vital Links: Canadian Cultural Industries.* Ministry of Supply and Services Canada. Ottawa. 1987. p. 7. This perception of Canadian culture owes much to the anthropological concept of culture proposed by Edward Burnett Tylor over a century ago. In his classic book on *The Origins of Culture* published in 1871, Tylor defined culture as *"that complex whole* which includes knowledge, belief, art, morals, custom, and any other capabilities and habits acquired by man as a member of society."￼ (Edward Burnett Tylor. *The Origins of Culture.* Harper and Row Publishers. New York. 1958. p. 1. [emphasis mine]).

[17] UNESCO. *Mexico City Declaration on Cultural Policies.* UNESCO. Paris. 1982.

Without neglecting the importance of creativity as expressed in intellectual and artistic activity, they [participants at the Mexico City Conference] considered it important to broaden the notion of culture to include behaviour patterns, the individual's view of him/herself, of society and of the outside world. In this perspective, the cultural life of a society may be seen to express itself through its way of living and being, through its perceptions and self-perceptions, its behaviour patterns, value systems and beliefs.[18]

Adoption of a holistic concept of Canadian culture could prove valuable and timely at this particular juncture in the country's history. Not only would it make it possible to see the country and its culture as a **whole** rather than as a series of fragmented and disconnected parts, but also it would make it possible to confront many of the country's most deep-seated problems and complex challenges — problems and challenges ranging all the way from the crisis of cultural identity and the need to maintain *cultural* sovereignty to the difficulties between Quebec and the rest of Canada and the quest for unity in diversity, surely the greatest cultural challenge facing Canada and Canadians of all. In so doing, it could provide a way of looking at and dealing with Canadian culture and the development of the country which transcends social, linguistic, regional, demographic, ethnic and geographical divisions and differences and is in keeping with the country's historical development, contemporary circumstances, present realities and future needs.

---

[18] UNESCO. *A Practical Guide to the World Decade for Cultural Development 1988-1997.* UNESCO. Paris. 1987. p. 16.

THE CONTENT OF CANADIAN CULTURE

> All people adopt or inherit a culture, an integral whole of accumulated resources, both material and non-material, which they utilize, transform and transmit in order to satisfy their needs, assert their identity and give meaning to their lives.
>
> Achoka Awori[1]

When Canadian culture is conceived and defined as a "whole" rather than as "a part of a whole," it is concerned with all aspects and dimensions of life and living in Canada. There is not a single event, experience, individual, institution, or group which is not affected, and affected deeply, by Canadian culture.

It is this fact which makes Canadian culture every Canadian's business. It is as much the concern of the farmer in Saskatchewan, the fisherman in Newfoundland and the logger in British Columbia as it is the concern of the businessman in Ontario, the artist in Quebec, the teacher in New Brunswick and the banker in the North West Territories. It cuts across every conceivable segment and sector of Canadian society, from agriculture, industry and the arts to commerce, government, wholesale and retail trade, recreation, education and the environment.

Visualized in this way, Canadian culture is a vast and complex field. It is intimately connected with, and inexorably linked to, every determinant and dimension of Canadian development. Not only does every Canadian have a valuable contribution to make to it, but also every Canadian has a fundamental stake in it.

When Canadian culture is visualized in this holistic way, it possesses a breadth, depth, complexity and vitality which goes far beyond most other fields. This breadth, depth, complexity and vitality can be depicted in the following schema. It is a schema designed to depict

---

[1]Achoka Awori. "Culture, Environment and Development: How?"

Canadian culture **as a whole** as well as a constellation of interrelated and interdependent parts, all duly situated in the larger natural and historical environment.

VISUALIZATION OF CANADIAN CULTURE

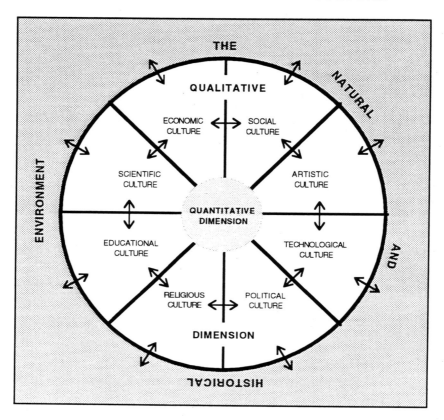

While Canadian culture embraces all aspects and dimensions of life and living in Canada, it hinges on six concerns which are of greatest importance and utmost urgency to Canada and Canadians at the present time as well as in the future. These concerns are:

- ***CANADIAN CULTURE AS A WHOLE***
  This is depicted in the schema as the largest circle because it represents the sum total of all the component parts of the country's culture — the economic culture, the social culture, the artistic culture, the educational culture and the like.

- **THE COMPONENT PARTS OF CANADIAN CULTURE**
  This is depicted in the schema as the separate sectors of Canadian culture, such as the economic culture, the political culture, the artistic culture, the educational culture and the like.

- **THE RELATIONSHIPS BETWEEN THE COMPONENT PARTS OF CANADIAN CULTURE**
  This is depicted in the schema as the arrows between the separate sectors or component parts of Canadian culture, such as the arrow between the economic culture and the scientific culture, or the arrow between the artistic culture and the technological culture.

- **THE RELATIONSHIPS BETWEEN THE COMPONENT PARTS OF CANADIAN CULTURE AND CANADIAN CULTURE AS A WHOLE**
  This is depicted in the schema as the arrows between the component parts of Canadian culture and the largest circle or Canadian culture as a whole.

- **THE RELATIONSHIP BETWEEN THE QUANTITATIVE AND QUALITATIVE DIMENSIONS OF CANADIAN CULTURE**
  This is depicted in the schema as the arrows between the lightly-shaded and unshaded areas or the qualitative and quantitative dimensions of the country's culture.

- **THE RELATIONSHIP BETWEEN CULTURE AS A WHOLE AND THE NATURAL AND HISTORICAL ENVIRONMENT**
  This is depicted in the schema as the relationship between the largest circle or Canadian culture as a whole and the vast expanse of space and time beyond Canadian culture or the natural and historical environment.

Since these six concerns comprise the sum and substance of Canadian culture when it is looked at as a whole, it pays to examine them in depth. For in combination they hold the key to unlocking the secrets of Canadian culture when it is visualized and dealt with as a totality.

BASIC CONCERNS OF CANADIAN CULTURE

As far as Canadian culture as a whole is concerned, it is clear that the principal task of Canadian development is to develop Canadian culture in a comprehensive, holistic sense. In order to do this, it is not only necessary to build up the component parts of Canadian culture — economic systems, political ideologies and processes, educational institutions, social programmes, technological and recreational practices, artistic and heritage activities, transportation and communications industries, religious and spiritual activities and the like — it is also necessary to achieve a dynamic and harmonious relationship between them. For only in this way can a culture be created which is capable of meeting the complex demands and multifarious challenges which are imposed on it.

While the principal task of Canadian development is to develop Canadian culture in this holistic sense, this is not possible without recognition of the fact that the country's culture is composed of many component parts. A very important aspect of Canadian development, therefore, involves developing the component parts of Canadian culture as specific or complex entities in their own right. Not only should they be developed in terms of their own material form and organic structure, but also they should be developed in terms of the excellence, creativity and ingenuity which comprises them.

Given the highly specialized nature of contemporary society, a great deal is already known about how to develop the component parts of Canadian culture, even if the financial, capital and human resources are not always available to achieve this. What is most interesting about the component parts of Canadian culture when Canadian culture is conceived and defined as a whole, however, is the fact that they all share culture in common. This explains why the component parts of the country's culture have been depicted in the schema as the artistic culture, the social culture, the economic culture, the political culture and the like since culture is the common thread which links them all together to form a whole. When artists and members of Canada's artistic community talk about culture being the substance which is needed to create "the ties that bind," it is this cohesive property in culture they have in mind. Without this, there is the ever-present danger that the country will become unglued and split apart.

While a great deal is known about the component parts of Canadian culture as entities in their own right, much less is known about the complex relationships which exist between and among them. For example, what is the relationship between the economic culture and the social culture, and how can this relationship be evolved most effectively in the future? Or what is the relationship between the artistic culture and the technological culture? How can technology be dealt with in such a way that it impacts favourably rather than unfavourably on the future development of the performing, exhibiting and creative arts? As these two illustrations demonstrate only too well, there is a series of complex relationships among the component parts of the country's culture which must be understood and dealt with if development is to evolve effectively in the future. Understanding these relationships is looming ever larger in the matrix of Canadian cultural concerns which must be addressed if Canadian development is to be attended to properly in the future.

Just as Canadian culture is concerned with the network of relationships which exist between and among the component parts of the country's culture, so it is concerned with the myriad relationships which exist between the component parts of Canadian culture and Canadian culture as a whole. Viewed from this perspective, the country's culture provides the **context** or **container** within which the component parts are situated and developed. This makes it imperative to focus attention on the dynamic interplay and interaction that is constantly going on between Canadian culture as a whole and the component parts which comprise it. For example, how are changes that are going on in the economy, politics, the arts and the sciences impacting on Canadian culture as a whole? And conversely, how are changes that are going on in Canadian culture as a whole impacting on the economy, politics, the arts and the sciences? Questions such as these are of crucial importance to Canada's present and future development.

Just as it is necessary to focus attention on the network of relationships which exist between the component parts of Canadian culture and Canadian culture as a whole, so it is necessary to focus attention on the relationship which exists between the qualitative and quantitative dimension of the country's culture. Of the two, it is the qualitative dimension that is the most difficult to deal with and pin down. This is because it cannot be touched, handled, exchanged or seen, and is virtually impossible to measure and define.

Subdividing Canadian culture into a qualitative dimension and a quantitative dimension makes it possible to shine the spotlight squarely on the material and non-material aspects of the country's culture, surely one of the most crucial and complex problems of Canada's development of all. How large should the quantitative dimension be compared to the qualitative dimension? And what should the relationship be between them?

It is obvious from the schema that the larger the quantitative dimension or material aspect of culture, the more pressure is exerted outward on the natural environment. Conversely, the smaller the quantitative dimension or material aspect, the less pressure is exerted outward on the natural environment. In other words, the more time and energy is spent on the production, distribution and consumption of material goods and commodities, the more pressure is exerted on nature and the less time and energy is available for social interaction, spiritual renewal, friendship, human love, recreation, re-creation and all those things which make life a fuller, richer and more meaningful affair. It is a situation that demands the greatest attention and discussion in the future because it is so intimately connected with the environmental crisis and the health, welfare and well-being of all Canadians.

This leads directly to the most important relationship of all, namely the relationship between Canadian culture and the natural and historical environment. Just as Canadian culture provides the context or container for the component parts of Canadian culture and the maze of relationships which exist between and among these component parts, so the natural and historical environment provides the context or container for Canadian culture as a whole. Careful scrutiny of this relationship is imperative if Canadian development is to be attended to properly in the future. For as history has confirmed time and again, cultures that are not properly contexted in the natural and historical environment run the perpetual risk of becoming unglued and splitting apart.

Viewed from this perspective, nothing could be more important to the development of Canadian culture in the future than situating the country's culture properly in the natural and historical environment. On the one hand, this means ensuring that Canada's cultural policies and practices are such that ecological well-being and environmental sustainability are assured, which will clearly be impossible without examining very carefully the impact that various types of cultural policies and practices have on the natural environment and natural resources. On the other hand, it means ensuring that interpretations of Canadian history are as honest and accurate as possible, and there is real recognition of the vital contributions that all Canadians have made and continue to make to Canadian development. Anything less than this will mean that Canadian culture is not positioned properly in the natural and historical environment or space and time.

THE ESSENCE OF CANADIAN CULTURE

Conceiving and defining Canadian culture as a whole rather than as part of a whole necessitates a quantum leap in consciousness with respect to the way Canadian culture is visualized, conceptualized, talked about, treated and dealt with in the future. Rather than thinking about and dealing with Canadian culture as a part of a whole or parts of a whole the way the official concept of Canadian culture does — and indeed any definition of Canadian culture does which defines the country's culture in specialized or partial rather than holistic terms — Canadian culture is thought about and dealt with as a whole in its own right. Thus, attention is shifted from the component parts of Canadian culture — which has traditionally been the case — to Canadian culture as a total, integrated entity. How is the whole structured and put together? What assumptions and axioms underlie it? How is it organized and arranged? And how is it positioned in the natural and historical environment or space and time? These are the fundamental questions which must be addressed at this particular juncture in the historical evolution of the country and its culture.

Visualized and articulated in this way, it is clear that Canadian development is concerned with two matters of quintessential importance when it is stripped to its essence. The first is **values**, or the specific weights or priorities which are accorded to the component parts of the country's culture as well as the country's culture as a whole. The second is **worldview**, or how the country's culture is structured and put together as well as how it is situated in the natural and historical environment or space and time.

The importance of values has long been recognized. More than two decades ago, a group of Canadian scholars assembled by the Canadian Commission for UNESCO came up with the following definition of culture and by implication Canadian culture:

> Culture is a dynamic value system of learned elements with assumptions, conventions, beliefs and rules permitting members of a group to relate to each other and to the world, to communicate and to develop their creative potential.[2]

Values are an essential part of Canadian culture because they are concerned with the way the diverse ingredients of Canadian culture are put together to form a whole. Jerzy Wojciechowski comments on the crucial importance of values in general and the hierarchy of values and value systems in particular in the formation of cultures:

> It should be pointed out that the hierarchy of values underlying each culture is the principle of internal cohesion

[2] Canadian Commission for UNESCO. *A Working Definition of Culture for the Canadian Commission for UNESCO.* Occasional Paper 26. Canadian Commission for UNESCO. Ottawa. 1977. p. 6.

of a culture, which bonds the various elements of a culture together and structures them into an organized whole composed of interdependent parts.[3]

In Canada's case, the country's "organized whole" is composed of myriads of interdependent and interrelated parts. While these parts may share certain similarities with the parts of other cultures, most notably American culture and several European cultures, the very fact that these parts have been woven together in different combinations, arrangements and proportions means that Canadian culture is distinctive and unique. Its distinctiveness and uniqueness derives from the fact that successive generations of Canadians — from the native peoples to the many diverse peoples which make up Canada's population today — have woven together the separate strands of the country's cultural life in such a way that the result is a tapestry which is without duplication elsewhere in the world. It is this fact which differentiates Canadian culture from American culture, French culture, British culture, or any other culture. While Canadians may watch similar television programmes to Americans and may have inherited certain ideas and ideals from Europeans and other peoples in the world, the very fact that Canadians have struggled against incredible odds over the centuries to create a distinctive and specific cultural life means that Canadian culture is significantly different from the cultures of other countries.

In part, the code that successive generations of Canadians have used to create this culture has not been of their own making. It has been imposed on them by the natural environment and other cultures, largely by virtue of the fact that Canada occupies a very distinctive piece of the world's geography and many immigrants to the country have brought with them values from other parts of the world which have been configured into the larger fabric of Canadian culture. However, in large measure, the code which successive generations of Canadians have used to create their unique and distinctive culture has been very much of their own making: it has been consciously and deliberately designed to meet the specific needs

---

[3] Jerzy A. Wojciechowski. "Cultural Pluralism and National Identity." in *Cultures*. Volume IV. No. 4. 1977. (Cultural Trends). UNESCO Press and La Baconnière. UNESCO. Paris. 1977. p. 54.

and concerns of Canadians for survival, security, material comfort, peace, order, decency and individual and collective well-being. These needs and concerns have always been, and probably will always be, key components in Canadian development. Recognition of this fact should cause Canadians to recognize that Canadian identity is not some elusive quality that must be achieved in the future. On the contrary, it already exists. It is recognized the moment attention is focused on Canadian culture *as a whole* and the struggle successive generations of Canadians have waged over the centuries to create this whole.

It is impossible to focus attention on Canadian culture as a whole without focusing attention on the "worldview" which underlies it. Here again, values in general and the hierarchy of values in particular play a pivotal role:

> The hierarchy of values underlying a culture integrates elements of knowledge into a world view, determines to a large extent attitudes and reactions to life situations, and offers a general framework for man's conscious presence in, and relationship to, the world. Central to each culture are convictions about the universe and about man, about his nature, his relation to the external world, his place in the universe, the meaning of human life, the supreme values, and the distinction between right and wrong, good and evil.
>
> The sum of these convictions forms in each case a unique and distinctive system, differing from culture to culture, even though some of its elements are similar in different cultures. It is this system which shapes the beliefs, attitudes and behaviour of individuals.[4]

Like values and value systems, Canada's worldview is derived from many different places and sources. Not only has it received contributions from a variety of locations and domains — foreign and domestic as well as historical and contemporary — but also it is a compilation of many different and diverse worldviews. This is understandable in view of the fact that the various people of Canada visualize and interpret the world somewhat differently. Thus, for example, Canadians of French background

---

[4] Jerzy A. Wojciechowski. "Cultural Pluralism and National Identity." *ibid.* p. 54.

visualize and interpret the world somewhat differently from Canadians of English background, who in turn visualize and interpret the world somewhat differently from the native peoples and Canadians of Italian, Greek, African, Asian, Caribbean or Latin American background. Realization of this fact highlights the fact that pressures and tensions between different groups of Canadians are inevitable because they see the world slightly differently and act in the world somewhat differently. And it highlights something else. It highlights the need for integration of the various worldviews which in combination make up Canada's total worldview.

The need for integration of the various worldviews which comprise Canada's total worldview underlines the need for dynamic change in the way Canadians visualize and interpret the world. Not only must there be constant adjustments in the component parts of Canadian culture and the complex interconnections and interrelationships which exist between and among these parts, but also there must be fundamental transformations in Canadian culture as a whole and the values and worldviews which underlie and shape this whole. Without this, Canadian culture will not be able to respond to the countless challenges and opportunities which confront it.

This is precisely why viewing Canadian culture *as a whole* proves so valuable. It provides a way of thinking about, looking at and dealing with the country's culture which transcends the interests of particular groups, specific regions and powerful lobbies and institutions. The focus is always on Canadian culture as a whole and the need to continuously transform and recreate this whole so that it is in the best possible position to confront new challenges and open up new opportunities. Ultimately this is what Canadian culture and Canadian development are all about.

THE REALITY OF CANADIAN CULTURE

> Because cultures are wholes, are systematic (composed of interrelated systems in which each aspect is functionally interrelated with all other parts), and are highly contexted as well, it is hard to describe them from the outside. A given culture cannot be understood simply in terms of content or parts. One has to know how the whole system is put together, how the major systems and dynamisms function, and how they are interrelated.
>
> Edward Hall[1]

For many Canadians, the problem is not how to define Canadian culture or determine its content, but rather how to **know** it. In other words, the problem is not with Canadian culture as a concept, but with Canadian culture as a reality.

Why is it necessary for Canadians to know their culture? It is necessary because it is through knowledge of the country's culture that Canadians get to know themselves, each other, the world around them and the threads which bind them together as a people. Moreover, it is through knowledge of Canadian culture that Canadians are able to distinguish and differentiate themselves from other peoples, particularly Americans and Europeans, as well as protect themselves from foreign cultural aggression and preserve their cultural integrity, identity and sovereignty.

KNOWLEDGE OF CANADIAN CULTURE

It is one thing to know Canadian culture when it is defined as the arts, heritage and cultural industries. It is quite another to know Canadian culture when it is defined **as a whole**.

When Canadian culture is defined as the arts, heritage and cultural industries, knowledge of the country's culture comes from objects, artefacts and presentations which can be seen, touched, experienced and

---

[1] Edward T. Hall. *Beyond Culture*. Anchor Press/Doubleday. Garden City. 1976. p. 195.

talked about. Plays can be enjoyed; books can be read; and television programmes and films can be watched. But when Canadian culture is defined as a whole, it can never be known or experienced in this material or physical sense. It is far too vast, complex, abstract and intangible for that.

How then is it possible to know Canadian culture? For Giles Gunn, an internationally-recognized cultural scholar and critic, the best place to start getting to know and understand a whole — any whole — is with the parts and especially the dynamic interplay that is constantly going on between the parts and the whole:

> We cannot understand the parts of anything without some sense of the whole to which they belong, just as we cannot comprehend the whole to which they belong until we have grasped the parts that make it up. Thus we are constantly obliged to move back and forth in our effort to understand something "between the whole conceived through the parts which actualize it and the parts conceived through the whole which motivates them."[2]

For Canadians anxious to know their culture as a whole, the process starts with their own specific part of the whole, such as their job, family, community, life, or geographical location in the country. But it is not their job, family, community, life or geographical location taken in isolation, but rather as part of the larger fabric of the culture of the country as a whole. In other words, it is the details of their own specific cultural situation considered in terms of the larger context of the country's overall cultural life.

While this does not provide the ultimate solution to the problem of getting to know Canadian culture, at least it starts the process moving in the right direction because it encourages Canadians to think about the larger container within which their own particular cultural experiences and circumstances are located.

---

[2] Giles Gunn. *The Culture of Criticism and the Criticism of Culture.* Oxford University Press. New York. 1987. p. 95.

To progress further, it is necessary to turn to the country's artists, scholars, critics, architects and other types of creative people. This is because artists, scholars, critics, architects and other types of creative people possess the intuitive and sensorial abilities which are needed to sense how Canadian culture as a whole is structured and put together, as well as the expressive and communicative capabilities which are needed to communicate vital information, insights, ideas and knowledge about the country's culture as a whole in their works.

Robert Redfield, a cultural anthropologist who spent his lifetime studying cultural and human wholes, comments on the unique ability artists, scholars, critics and other types of creative people possess to pass on knowledge and understanding about a whole as a whole, compared to those who possess ability to pass on knowledge and understanding about the parts of a whole:

> Still farther from where we just now stand are those who study the relations of parts to parts, of elements abstracted out from the whole in strict and limited relationship to each other... They are those who make a science from chosen parts of human wholes, placed in relation to other such parts, but not in relation to all the parts of the original whole....
>
> Over there, on that other side, are all those who strive to present the concrete reality of each human whole as each, in itself, is. They are a various group. Included are novelists, philosophers, historians, philosophers of history, literary people, critics of literature and of art, historians of art and writers of personal reminiscences. These people describe human wholes — personalities, civilizations, epochs, literatures, local cultures — each in its uniqueness.[3]

This ability to convey vital information, insights, ideas and knowledge about cultures as "wholes" places artists, scholars, critics, architects and other types of creative people in a position of crucial importance to society. Through their use of myths, metaphors, signs,

---

[3] Robert Redfield. *The Little Community: Viewpoints for the Study of the Human Whole.* The University of Chicago Press. Chicago. 1973. pp. 158-159.

symbols, similes, allegories, anomalies, analogies and the like, artists, scholars, critics, architects and other types of creative people create the content which is necessary to communicate a vast amount of information and understanding about cultures as wholes which simply cannot be passed on in any other way. The old adage, "a picture is worth a thousand words" is a trite cliché, but it speaks volumes about the ability of these types of people to communicate an incredible amount of knowledge, information and understanding about cultures as wholes which simply cannot be communicated at all in any other way, or cannot be communicated as effectively using any other device.

Robert Redfield calls this "the ability for portraiture." It is an ability that artists posses in abundance:

> The characterizations of the artist...are of course not precise at all; but very much of the whole is communicated to us. We might call them all portraits. They communicate the nature of the whole by attending to the uniqueness of each part, by choosing from among the parts certain of them for emphasis, and by modifying them and rearranging them in ways that satisfy the "feeling" of the portrayer....
>
> In the portraiture accomplished by art, exaggerations, distortions, and substitutions of one sort or another play important parts. Caricature and satire are special forms of portraiture. *Each describes the whole by overemphasizing something felt to be significantly true of the whole.* Metaphors and analogy offer different and parallel images for understanding the whole, as does the parable: a narrative standing for a human something other than itself.[4]

It is this capacity that is not well understood in Canadian society at the present time. For in the act of communicating vital information about cultures as wholes, artists and other types of creative people not only strip cultures to their fundamental principles and lay bare their essence, *they also help people to order their cultural universe.* Edward Hall, one of

---

[4] Robert Redfield. *The Little Community: Viewpoints for the Study of the Human Whole.* The University of Chicago Press. Chicago. 1973. pp. 161-162. (emphasis mine).

the world's foremost authorities on cultural communication,[5] explains why this is so:

> It is the artist's task to remove obstacles that stand between his audience and the events he describes. In so doing, he abstracts from nature those parts which, if properly organized, can stand for the whole and constitute a more forceful, uncluttered statement than the layman might make for himself. In other words, **one of the principal functions of the artist is to help the layman order his cultural universe.**[6]

The implications of this for Canada, Canadians and Canadian culture are clear and unequivocal. It is the function of Canadian artists and the arts generally to help Canadians know, understand and experience their culture as a whole. In so doing, they make it possible for Canadians to know themselves, each other, their surroundings, their purpose and philosophy of life, their values, their worldview, their relations with other countries, their position in the world and their association with the natural environment. This vaults Canadian artists and the arts generally into a position of crucial importance in Canadian society. Without systematic and sustained exposure to the arts and Canadian artistic works, Canadians will never get to know, understand or experience their culture as a whole.

While Canadian artists perform this "holistic function" most effectively, they are not the only people to perform this function. As indicated earlier, scholars, architects, historians, philosophers, critics and other types of creative people also perform this function. By deliberately selecting parts of the whole to stand for the whole and focusing attention *on the picture itself rather than on the individual pieces which make up the picture*, scholars, architects, historians, philosophers, critics and other types of creative people broaden and

---

[5] See, for example, Edward Hall. *The Silent Language.* Anchor Books. Anchor Press/Doubleday. Garden City. 1973; Edward Hall. *The Hidden Dimension.* Doubleday and Company, Inc. Garden City. 1966; Edward Hall. *Beyond Culture.* Anchor Press/Doubleday. Garden City. 1976.

[6] Edward Hall. *The Hidden Dimension.* ibid. p. 74.

deepen Canadians' knowledge, understanding and experience of their culture as a dynamic, interrelated and organic entity.

It is clear from this that Canada's artists, scholars, historians, philosophers and critics have a valuable role to play in the piecing together of a comprehensive portrait of Canadian culture as a whole. For it is through the works of painters such as Clarence Gagnon, Cornelius Kreighoff, Jean-Paul Riopelle, Paul-Émile Borduas, William Kurelek, Emily Carr and the Group of Seven, composers such as Harry Freedman, Violet Archer and R. Murray Schafer, playwrights such as Lescarbot, Michel Tremblay, Tomson Highway and Sharon Pollock, poets such as Bliss Carman, Dorothy Livesay and Dennis Lee, architects such as Douglas Cardinal, Raymond Moriyama and Arthur Erickson, writers such as Margaret Laurence, Antonine Maillet, Margaret Atwood and Gabrielle Roy, historians such as Harold Innis, Pierre Berton and A.R.M. Lower, thinkers such as Marshall McLuhan, George Grant, Hugh MacLennan and Northrop Frye — as well as the works of many other Canadian artists, scholars, historians, architects, philosophers and critics too numerous to cite here — that a comprehensive portrait of Canadian culture starts to take shape. It is a portrait which differs significantly from the portrait of American culture, British culture, French culture or any other culture in its overall composition, basic features and fundamental design.

Unfortunately, the indispensable role that Canadian artists, scholars, historians, architects, philosophers, critics and other types of creative people play in the process of helping Canadians to see, know and understand their culture is not well understood by Canadians and the country's political, bureaucratic, corporate, educational and professional leaders. If it was, Canadians in general and Canada's governments, corporations, educational institutions and foundations in particular would be increasing rather than decreasing their financial and non-financial commitments to the arts and scholarship. Far too little understood is the fact that the country's creative talents are far more than providers of entertainment or generators of economic activity. They are vital and valuable contributors to the fund of knowledge, understanding and experience which is essential if Canadians are to "know their culture." No amount of performances, exhibitions or presentations of non-Canadian works will act as a substitute for this.

It is for reasons such as these that Canadian governments, corporations, foundations, educational institutions, and Canadians generally should be investing far more heavily in the arts, architecture, scholarship, historicism and criticism in general and the works of Canadian artists, architects, scholars, historians, philosophers and critics in particular. For these are the types of people and forms of cultural expression which speak most forthrightly and directly to Canadians about the way in which they visualize and interpret the world, organize themselves, conduct their affairs, elevate and enrich life, position themselves in the world and organize and orchestrate their cultural life. There is not one aspect of the country's culture which is not affected — and affected deeply — by the works of these talented people. Is there any job or task that is more essential to the country and its citizenry at the present time than this? The very future of the country may depend on it.

PORTRAIT OF CANADIAN CULTURE AS A WHOLE

Now that the problem of ascertaining how it is possible to know Canadian culture has been dealt with, it is possible to commence the process of piecing together a comprehensive portrait of the country's culture using the works of Canadian artists, scholars, critics, architects, historians and other types of creative people as a guide.

What stands out most clearly when Canadian culture is looked at as a whole is the fact that Canadian culture is a *northern culture*. There is hardly a single aspect of the country's cultural life which is not affected by this simple but undeniable fact.

When artists like the Group of Seven, David Milne, Doris McCarthy, Pitseolak, Emily Carr and others take Canadians into the far reaches of Canadian geography, they are reminding Canadians that they live in a culture that is extremely northern in nature and character. It is a culture that is not only strongly influenced by the trials and tribulations of climate and geography, but also keenly affected by the challenges of space and the environment. It is not coincidental that the most frequently heard comments about the work of the Group of Seven — quite apart from how magnificently they have captured the Canadian landscape — is how few people there are in their paintings. For the awesomeness of Canada's environment, particularly when it is combined with the country's small population, means that Canada has one of the lowest people-to-land ratios in the world. It is a fact that Canada shares in common with several other northern cultures, such as the cultures of Greenland, Iceland, the Scandinavian countries, Russia and Mongolia.

What makes Canadian culture a decidedly northern culture is the character and quality of the landscape. For landscape, defined here to include geography, climate, location, terrain, flora and fauna and distinctive features, enters into the collective consciousness of Canadians and affects the way they visualize and interpret the world and act in the world.

What makes landscape such a powerful factor in shaping Canadian culture is its sheer size, sparseness, diversity, complexity and relative inhospitality. Whereas many countries are geographically quite contained, Canada stretches across some ten thousand kilometres and five and a half of the world's twenty-four time zones. While most of the land along the American border is rich and fertile, much of the land farther north is rugged and arduous. When this fact is combined with the fact that many parts of Canada are covered in snow for a significant part of the year, it is easy to see why size and physical terrain play such an important role in making Canadian culture a distinctly northern culture.

As important as size and physical terrain are, it is probably climate that plays the decisive role. Whereas many countries have two seasons — "wet season" and "dry season" — Canada has four seasons — winter, spring, summer and fall. While these seasons give Canadian culture a decidedly seasonal character, affecting employment patterns, recreational pursuits, economic activities and virtually everything else, it is not really the fact that Canada has four seasons that makes climate the decisive factor in shaping the northern nature of the country's culture. Rather it is the fact that these seasons tend to be dominated by one season, namely winter. Not only does winter tend to overpower all the other seasons, but Canadians are perpetually haunted by thoughts of winter even on the hottest and most oppressive days of summer.

When all these facts are combined, it is easy to understand why Canadians have such an intimate association with the natural environment. It is an association which can never be taken for granted and about which there is a great deal of ambivalence. On the one hand, there is the love of nature and the natural environment which Canadians manifest as a result of their appreciation of the sheer size, grandeur and beauty of the country, the great transformations which take place from season to season, the limitless recreational possibilities, the pristine state of much of the country's geography, and the endless expanse of land which is virtually unknown in many other cultures. On the other hand, there is the hatred of nature and the natural environment which Canadians manifest in terms of the ruthless exploitation and spoilation of the country's natural resources as well as the incredible hardships Canadians are compelled to endure as a result of the environment's challenging and often inhospitable nature.

It is the challenging and inhospitable nature of the country's environment that has led some of Canada's best-known and most-revered artists to depict Canadians as victims of a nasty trick perpetrated by nature. This has led to the conclusion that Canadians have been so terrorized by the harshness, cruelty and inhospitality of the environment that they identify more with the hunted than the hunter, the animal than the human. Others counter that it is the very fact that Canadians have confronted the environment and endured that gives Canadians a heroic quality — a heroic quality which makes it necessary to view Canadians as victors rather than vanquished, hunter rather than hunted. Regardless of which argument is accepted, there can be little doubt that the intense encounter which Canadians have waged over the centuries with a colossal piece of the world's geography casts a gigantic shadow over every aspect of Canadian cultural life. Whether it is Suzanna Moodie, Louis Hémon or

Catherine Parr Traill writing about the trials and tribulations of another harsh Canadian winter, Robert Bateman, Freeman Patterson or Glen Loates depicting the trauma and tragedy of the country's diminishing animal life, or the Group of Seven capturing the resplendent sights and smells of a spring meadow or fall forest, all Canadians are fully aware of the extent to which the country's northern climate and geography figure in the making and shaping of their culture as a whole.

It is the demands of this climate and geography which make survival a constant concern for Canadians.

In a very fundamental sense, survival is a basic concern of people in all cultures. Since nature seldom gives up its bounty without intense hardship, people in every culture are compelled to spend a significant part of their time worrying about survival and working to deal with it. Not only are there difficult decisions to be made about food supply, clothing, shelter and accommodation, but also there is the never-ending problem of the future, particularly in a world characterized by increased instability, uncertainty and loss of security.

But survival takes on a much more profound and pressing meaning in a northern culture like Canada's. In a culture where climate can play havoc with the distribution of food supplies, communications can be totally disrupted at any time, wind can cream off a farmer's topsoil in the split of a second and people can freeze to death in the cold, survival takes a very special significance. Just as it is impossible to escape thoughts of winter on the hottest days of summer, so it is impossible to escape thoughts of survival regardless of how much food is stocked in the larder and how many overcoats are hanging in the closet. Margaret Atwood explains why Canadians are so preoccupied — indeed obsessed — with survival:

> But the main idea is the first one: hanging on, staying alive. Canadians are forever taking the national pulse like doctors at a sickbed: the aim is not to see whether the patient will live well but simply whether he will live at all. Our central idea is one which generates, not the excitement and sense of

adventure or danger which The Frontier holds out, not the smugness and/or sense of security, of everything in its place, which The Island can offer, but an almost intolerable anxiety. Our stories are likely to be tales not of those who made it but of those who made it back, from the awful experience — the North, the snowstorm, the sinking ship — that killed everyone else.[7]

It is the fact that Canadian culture is a northern culture which gives rise to the constant concern with the material prerequisites which are necessary for survival. It is impossible to live in a northern culture without acquiring all the material accoutrements and technological necessities which are imperative for this. Whereas the material demands and dictates of southern cultures can often be considerably less, the material demands and dictates of northern cultures are often quite excessive. Boots, galoshes, parkas, scarves, mitts, many changes of clothing, elaborate heating systems, snowmobiles, insulated buildings, enclosed malls and underground walkways — which are unknown in southern cultures and warmer climates — are standard fare in northern cultures. This makes it difficult, and often quite misleading, to compare northern and southern cultures in terms of their consumption of energy, fossil fuels, electricity or products requiring a high degree of material input.

This should not be taken to mean that high levels of material consumption in a northern culture like Canada's should be condoned. Like people generally throughout the western world, Canadians have become heavy consumers of material resources and products in the post-war era, thereby making it imperative to examine very carefully where the material demands and dictates of a northern culture like Canada's end and the materialistic appetites of a consumer society begin. For as environmentalists and ecologists have been pointing out for decades, environmental collapse is inevitable if people in highly industrialized cultures do not curb their material appetites and bring their consumption practices under control.

---

[7] Margaret Atwood. *Survival*. Anansi. Toronto. 1972. p. 33.

It is the material requirements of Canadians which help to explain why Canadian culture is not only a northern culture, but also a *resource culture*. For in the process of coping with the demands and dictates of survival, a colossal geography, a demanding climate and an inhospitable environment, Canadians have been compelled to cultivate the natural resources of the country to the utmost.

Whereas artists like the Group of Seven and Margaret Atwood use landscape, geography and concern for survival to lay bare the fact that Canadian culture is a northern culture, historians like Harold Innis and Donald Creighton used the fact that Canadians are extremely dependent on natural resources to expose the resource nature of the country's culture.

By deliberately selecting two resources on which Canadians have been so dependent over a long period of historical time — fish and fur[8] — Innis was able to show how development and exploitation of two resources in particular and development and exploitation of natural resources in general impacted on every single aspect of Canadian cultural life. For Canada's natural resources are far more than economic resources. They are cultural resources in the fullest sense of the term because they give rise to an entire way of life which extends well beyond the economy and the development of the economic resources of the country to encompass human settlement, education and training, transportation and communications, social and family life, relationships with other countries, and the whole way Canadians visualize and interpret the world and act in the world. Thus, by deliberately selecting two specific parts of the whole to stand for the whole, Innis was able to show how dependency on natural resources not only dominates a significant part of Canada's cultural history, it also speaks volumes about Canadian culture and the actions and behaviour of Canadians as a whole. Viewed from this perspective, Canada is much more than a "resource economy." It is a "resource culture."

---

[8] Harold Innis. *The Fur Trade in Canada: An Introduction to Canadian Economic History.* University of Toronto Press. Toronto. 1930. Harold Innis. *The Cod Fisheries: The History of an International Economy.* University of Toronto Press. Toronto. 1940.

It is the peculiarities of the country's ecological circumstances and natural resource requirements which explains why Canadians are so dependent on the bounties of nature. For while these bounties are spread liberally across the length and breadth of the country, they have not given up their largesse without intense and relentless struggle. The enormous hardships which earlier generations of Canadians were compelled to endure to cultivate and develop these resources are legendary.

While some Canadians lament the fact that Canadians have been "hewers of wood and drawers of water" throughout much of their history and others complain that Canada and Canadians are too dependent on the resources of nature, who is not exceedingly grateful to past generations for toiling under conditions of extreme hardship to bring the natural resources of the country under cultivation. Moreover, who is not exceedingly grateful that Canada possesses a generous supply of natural resources — wood, water, precious metals, and perhaps most of all, land — in an age characterized by growing shortages of renewable and non-renewable resources, rapidly-escalating world population and growing spatial and physical constraints. While Canadians must remain ever watchful and mindful of their dependency on natural resources, particularly at a time when prices for natural resources are fluctuating and much of the processing of these resources takes place outside Canada, there is no doubt that the economic and non-economic rewards of a resource culture are quite substantial and will be even more so in the future.

It is the fact that Canadian culture is a resource culture which explains why collaboration and co-operation have been such a prominent feature of Canadian cultural life. For without collaboration and co-operation between citizens, corporations and governments in particular, and the public sector and the private sector in general, cultivating the natural resources of the country would not have been possible.

Unlike the United States, Great Britain and France where a much different economic situation and ecological configuration produced accumulations of capital and entrepreneurial capabilities which made it possible for citizens and commercial organizations to operate independently of governments and the political process, in Canada no such mode of action was possible. The demographic, ecological and economic reality of Canada was such that governments, corporations, entrepreneurs, commercial companies and private citizens were compelled to collaborate on the development of every conceivable enterprise of any significant size or stature. Whether it has been the creation of natural resource industries and companies, the construction of railroads and canals, the erection of a national communications system, the establishment of co-operatives and the co-operative movement, or the creation of medicare and social programmes, private entrepreneurs, corporations and citizens have been compelled to collaborate and work closely together with governments to generate the capital and commercial wherewithal which is necessary to reap the advantages of a resource culture.

It is the need for collaboration and co-operation which helps to explain why Canadians have a world-wide reputation for compromise and concession. For it is through collaboration and co-operation that Canadians have slowly but surely learned to adapt, adjust and get along.

It is an ability which has demonstrated itself time and again on both the domestic and international front. On the domestic front, it has manifested itself in the ability to work together and make concessions and compromises, despite the obvious geographical, regional, social and linguistic barriers and differences which separate the country and its citizenry. It is this co-operative ability which accounts for the fact that the country's mixed free-enterprise economic system and judiciously-designed political system — despite past problems and present challenges — is based on a delicate balancing of the forces of centralization and decentralization, localism, regionalism and federalism. However, it is really on the international scene where the capacity for collaboration, co-operation and compromise is most conspicuous. It has led to a solid reputation for Canada in bilateral and multilateral relations and world affairs as a conciliator, peace-maker, peace-keeper and respecter of people's basic rights and freedoms.

If collaboration and co-operation is one feature of Canada's resource culture, decentralization is another. Whereas collaboration and co-operation have been necessary to generate the funds which have been required to cultivate the natural resources of the country, decentralization has been necessary because the resources of the country are dispersed over such a wide variety of diverse locations and different terrains.

In a country where population distribution and human settlement have followed the location and availability of resources, it did not take long for Canada's highly decentralized demographic and ecological pattern to evolve and take shape. The northern nature of the country and the material needs of Canadians necessitated the sprinkling of small pockets of population over the gigantic land mass whenever and wherever resources were available and the environment proved susceptible to settlement. Not only has this produced a culture which is highly decentralized in every aspect and dimension of its cultural life, but also it has resulted in a culture which has one of the lowest people-to-land ratios in the world. In contrast to cultures which are highly centralized by virtue of the fact that they occupy a small land mass or possess a large population, Canadian culture is highly decentralized because the natural resources of the country are spread liberally over Canada's gigantic land mass and the population of the country is small compared to the populations of many other countries.

This high degree of decentralization has been at the core of many of Canada's most complex challenges and debilitating problems. Many of the challenges and problems Canadians face at the present time in terms of cultural identity, sovereignty and survival, for example, emanate from the fact that it is difficult to keep Canadians together and in communication across such a gigantic land mass. This situation is exacerbated, as every Canadian knows only too well, by the natural contours of North American geography which tend to run north-south rather than east-west. This has not only made it difficult for Canadians to maintain communications and stay in touch, it has also presented innumerable political problems. These problems are evident across the entire spectrum of political activity, from the federal level right down to the municipal level. Is Canada a "community of communities," a "federation of provinces," a "constellation of regions," an "assembly of nations," or a "nation state?" Opinions vary markedly across the country. On the one hand, there are those who believe that despite the fact that Canada's political system is highly decentralized, it is not decentralized enough. Proponents of this view contend that much more emphasis should be placed on community and regional development; and that municipal and provincial governments should be given much more power, responsibility and taxation authority to address local needs. On the other hand, there are those who contend that the problem with the country is that it is too decentralized and needs to be much more centralized. The country's political problems and identity and sovereignty requirements will never be met, so the argument goes, without a strong federal government. Such a government must have the powers, authority and resources to keep the country and its citizenry together when geographical and demographic forces are conspiring to split them apart. This makes finding the right admixture of centralization and decentralization — or federalism, regionalism and localism — as difficult a problem as finding the proper balance between materialism and non-materialism. Indeed, these twin problems are looming larger and larger in the overall matrix of cultural concerns which must be successfully attended to and addressed in the future.

If Innis' classic studies on the fur trade, cod fisheries and Canada's dependence on natural resources and staple production generally were instrumental in shedding light on the fact that Canadian culture is a resource culture, they were also instrumental in shedding light on the fact that Canadian culture is a *communications culture.*

All cultures are communications cultures in the sense that they depend on various types of communications — oral, verbal, non-verbal, mechanical, technological and so forth — to bind people together in space and time. Nevertheless, communications has a special significance for Canada and Canadians. This is because Canada is flung across such a vast expanse of geography. It is far from coincidental that Innis turned later in life to the study of communications as a unifying theme in history,[9] or that Marshall McLuhan, perhaps the greatest proponent of communications of all, is Canadian.

In retrospect, it is clear why Innis was driven to the conclusion that communications systems in general and modes of communication in particular are unifying themes in history and principal determinants of cultural life. As his studies on the development of staples industries and communication systems intensified, it became clear that the development of the fur trade, the cod fisheries, the timber trade and the wheat industry would not have been possible without the erection of an elaborate system of communications — a system capable of confronting Canada's complex and complicated communications problems.

It is the colossal size of the country and the resource-based nature of the country's culture which has made it imperative for Canadians to constantly create new communications technologies. For without the development of new communications technologies, the movement of people, products, ideas and information across the far-flung reaches of Canadian geography would not have been possible.

In earlier centuries, there were the snowshoes, dogsleds, kayaks, canoes, long boats, shipping systems and especially railroads which were imperative for penetration into the interior of the country and the movement of trappers, lumberjacks, farmers, merchants, fish, fur, timber, wheat and precious metals over long distances. In the twentieth century, there have been all those developments in contemporary communications — telegraph and telephone networks, radio, television and broadcasting systems, extraterrestrial satellites, electronic highways, information networks and the like — which have been designed to keep Canadians in touch and move people, products, information and ideas from one end of the country to the other.

---

[9] Harold Innis. *The Bias of Communications.* University of Toronto Press. Toronto. 1951. Also see, Harold Innis. *The Strategy of Culture.* University of Toronto Press. Toronto. 1952.

Viewed from this perspective, it is easy to see why communications has often been dubbed "the lifeblood" of Canadian culture. For without the capacity to link the country together and stay in touch, Canada as a country and Canadians as a people would be inconceivable. Not only would the country quickly disintegrate into a heterogeneous mass of provinces, regions and communities with distinctively different interests and agendas, but Canadians would find that they have less and less in common and have a harder and harder time keeping the country together and staying in touch.

More than anyone else, it was McLuhan who made Canadians and the world aware of the quintessential role that communications play in shaping cultures.[10] Building on the seminal theories and ideas developed by Innis, McLuhan demonstrated that modern communications in general and electronic communications in particular are transforming the nature of national and international relations, creating a "global village," and rewriting centuries-old cultural and communications patterns and traditions. Not only is form triumphing over content according to McLuhan — "the medium is the message" was McLuhan's euphemism for it — but also different media have different centralizing, decentralizing and engagement possibilities. Media become "hot" and "cold" and "centralizing" and "decentralizing" according to the communications properties that are inherent in them.

Given the enormous power of contemporary communications, it will not be possible to keep Canadians and Canadian culture together and in touch without an indigenous communications capability and the ability to maintain control over it. Viewed from this perspective, the degree of American control and ownership of Canada's current communications systems and media capabilities must be viewed as a cause for concern. Not only are most of Canada's cultural industries owned and operated by Americans — anywhere from sixty to ninety percent depending on whether

---

[10] Marshall McLuhan. *The Gutenberg Galaxy*. University of Toronto Press. Toronto. 1962. Marshall McLuhan. *The Technological Bride*. Saunders. Toronto. 1968. Marshall McLuhan. *Understanding Media*. McGraw-Hill. Toronto. 1964. Also see Arthur Kroker. *Technology and the Canadian Mind: Innis/McLuhan/Grant*. New World Perspectives. Montreal. 1984.

it is publishing, film, broadcasting or recording — but also most of the films and television programmes which Canadians watch are American.[11] Thus, as Canada moves progressively into the information age — an age dominated by electronic communications and information highways — it will not be sufficient to continuously create new communications technologies. It will also be necessary to ensure that communications systems and media capabilities are in Canadian rather than foreign hands and are operated with the interests of Canada and Canadians at heart.

If Canadian culture is a communications culture by virtue of the fact that Canada is well-wired with communications technology and Canadians own an incredible amount of communications gadgetry in per capita terms, it is also a *diverse culture.* This diversity manifests itself in every domain of the country's cultural life.

Take the economy as an example. While the economies of many countries are highly specialized and focused on a few well-defined areas, Canada's economy is highly diversified and spread across the entire spectrum of primary, secondary and tertiary production and distribution. And what is true for the economy is equally true for the educational system and social programmes. Not only is Canada's educational system highly diversified from coast to coast with a vast array of different courses, programmes, specialties and opportunities, but also the country's social programmes are highly diversified as well, with an incredible admixture of funding arrangements, granting procedures, transfer payments and the like. While there are periodic cries for rationalization of the country's social and educational systems along more national and uniform lines, who would deny the fact that these systems reflect the high degree of diversity which is evident throughout Canada today.

While this high degree of diversity manifests itself everywhere in the country, it is probably in the demographic domain that it is most conspicuous. Not only is Canada's population exceedingly diversified and

---

[11] Department of Communications. *Vital Links: Canadian Cultural Industries.* Ministry of Supply and Services. Ottawa. 1987. Also see, Paul Audley. *Canada's Cultural Industries: Broadcasting, Publishing, Records and Film.* Canadian Institute for Economic Policy. Ottawa. 1983.

varied, but also Canada is truly a multicultural and multiracial society characterized by many different peoples and diverse ethnic groups.[12] Moreover, it is getting more and more multicultural and multiracial all the time. While this poses difficult problems for Canada and Canadians in terms of intercultural communication and racial understanding, it also produces numerous opportunities in terms of exposure to different cultures and diverse cultural customs, values and traditions. With the recent influx of immigrants from Asia, Africa, Latin America, the Middle East and the Caribbean, it is possible to experience salient features of every culture in the world without leaving the shores of Canada.

For some, Canada's current policy of multiculturalism is one of the greatest assets of the country. Rather than forcing people to assimilate into one huge and homogeneous "melting pot," much as American culture has done, Canadian culture enables people from many different parts of the world and cultural backgrounds to maintain their traditions and identity. For others, however, the current policy of multiculturalism represents a serious liability, since it recognizes so many different cultural beliefs, practices, conventions and customs that it makes Canadian unity impossible.

It has been the willingness of the French and the English to **search** for unity through diversity and integration rather than uniformity and assimilation which has given rise to the current policy of multiculturalism and the intermingling of peoples with vastly different values, traditions, customs and beliefs. It is a struggle which has been fraught with tensions and difficulties from the outset, as the various constitutional battles and linguistic difficulties reveal. Nevertheless, it is a struggle that is as imperative as it is necessary. There is something about uniformity, assimilation and homogenization that is as oppressive as it is uninspiring.

It is the highly diverse nature of Canadian culture which makes Canadian culture a *dynamic culture*. Whereas many cultures are relatively

---

[12] John Burnet. *Coming Canadians: An Introduction to a History of Canadian Peoples.* McClelland & Stewart. Toronto. 1988.

conservative and static, changing very little from generation to generation and century to century, Canadian culture is a dynamic culture by virtue of the fact that it is in a constant state of flux as old ways of doing things change and new ways of doing things are opened up.

This dynamic quality has been a characteristic feature of Canadian culture from the outset. It manifested itself in the cultural initiatives and experiences of the native peoples as they moved from west to east across the country in search for food, clothing and shelter. It manifested itself in the early explorations and activities of the French and the English as they scoured the continent looking for fish, fur, food, precious metals and favourable signs of accommodation and settlement. It manifested itself in the pioneering accomplishments of the early settlers as they struggled to come to grips with the rudiments of a northern geography and the trials and tribulations of a cold climate. And it manifests itself today in the cultural patterns, rhythms and themes which Canadians trace out on a daily basis as they attempt to adjust to the rapidly-changing global reality. In all these periods, the country's culture has exhibited a dynamic quality which places it at or near the forefront of international cultural development and change.

If Canadian culture is a dynamic culture, it is also a *creative culture*. In fact, creativity is probably the most characteristic feature of Canadian culture of all when it is looked at as a whole.

Like Canadian culture's diversity and dynamism, Canadian culture's creativity is manifested in every domain of the country's cultural life. For example, in transportation, there are numerous examples of Canadian cultural creativity and Canada's seminal contributions to the history of land, water, air and space travel, including the kayak, the canoe, the long boat, the dogsled, the snowmobile, the bush plane and many other types of conveyances. In habitation and settlement, there are all the modes of accommodation which Canadians have evolved over the centuries to cope with the adversities and uncertainties of a northern geography and cold climate, including the igloo, the tepee, the longhouse, indoor shopping malls, subterranean passageways, pedestrian walkways and various other types of urban and rural architecture. In the extraction industries, there are prodigious achievements in hydro-electricity, mining, engineering, newsprint production and petrochemical refining. And in communications, undoubtedly Canada's most fertile field of ingenuity and innovation, there are countless contributions to the development of the wireless, the telephone, the radio, film, video, television, telecommunications, photography, computer graphics and satellite communications. While Canada cannot lay claim to seminal contributions in all of these areas, it is amazing how many of them either commenced in Canada or Canadians played an instrumental role bringing them to fruition, even if they did not always possess the capital resources or entrepreneurial expertise to take commercial advantage of them.[13] It could scarcely be otherwise. For the dictates of a vast geography and decidedly northern climate have demanded a highly creative response to these formidable challenges. If necessity is the mother of invention, surely it has manifested itself profusely in the Canadian case.

This completes the portrait of Canadian culture when it is viewed and visualized as a whole. Predicated on and evolving naturally out of the specific experiences of Canada and the insights and works of Canada's artists, architects, scholars, historians, philosophers and critics, it is the portrait of a culture which is distinctly northern, diverse, dynamic and creative in character, as well as highly decentralized and oriented towards nature, natural resources, the natural environment and communications. While many or all of these characteristics may be discernible in other cultures, no other culture possesses them all, or possesses them to the same degree, to produce a culture that is in any way similar to Canadian culture. It is in this sense that Canadian culture is distinctive and unique.

CANADA'S WORLDVIEW AND VALUES

With this portrait of Canadian culture clearly in mind, it is possible to delve deeper into what makes Canadian culture distinctive and unique.

---

[13] J.J. Brown. *Ideas in Exile: A History of Canadian Inventions.* McClelland & Stewart. Toronto. 1967.

In order to do this, it is necessary to examine Canada's worldview and values. For if Canadian culture is different from the cultures of other countries, it is because Canadians have a specific way of looking at the world and valuing things in the world.

While geography, climate and the environment have played a forceful role in shaping Canada's worldview and values, an even more forceful role has been played by Canadians themselves. For in the process of building a unique and distinctive culture, Canadians have evolved a way of looking at the world and acting in the world which, while it shares certain similarities with other cultures in general and the American and European cultures in particular, is distinctively and uniquely Canadian.

The reason for this is that successive generations of Canadians have struggled against incredible odds to build a culture capable of responding to the specific needs, fears, hopes, dreams, insecurities and aspirations of Canadians for survival, security, material comfort, social well-being and personal and collective fulfilment. In the process, Canadians have slowly but surely evolved a worldview and value system that is different from the worldviews and value systems of other cultures, particularly with respect to the way people relate to each other, the functioning of the state, attitudes towards social security and health care, interactions between the public sector and the private sector, and geopolitical positioning and diplomatic relations in the world.

To say that Canada's worldview and value system is different from the worldviews and value systems of other cultures is not to say that the worldviews and value systems of other cultures have had no impact or influence on the development of Canada's worldview and value system. Obviously western worldviews and value systems in general, and western attitudes towards religion, the meaning of life and death, the creation and functioning of the universe and the importance of industry, effort, frugality and thrift, have had a profound impact on Canada's worldview and value system. What gives Canada's worldview and value system its distinctive and unique character, however, is the fact that Canadians have taken outlooks on the world and value systems from other cultures and parts of the world and moulded them to suit their own specific circumstances and needs.

What are some of the more conspicuous characteristics of the country's worldview and value system? While there is no general consensus on this and many of these issues are being hotly debated and keenly contested in Canada at the present time, some of the most conspicuous characteristics of Canada's worldview and value system appear to be: a belief in the orderly and systematic nature of the universe; a belief in the superiority of human beings over nature and other species; a belief in the capacity of human beings to control nature and turn it to their collective advantage; a belief in the progressive development of societies; a belief in rationality, practicality, hard work, honesty, integrity, parsimony and thrift; a commitment to justice, equality, fair play, civility, politeness, democracy, freedom and individualism; and a belief in caring, compassion and respect for the rights and freedoms of others. While many of these characteristics are linked to European and American values, attitudes and traditions, the fact that Canadians have tailored them to their own specific needs and circumstances makes Canada's worldview and value system very distinctive and unique.

This fact is apparent as soon as Canada's worldview and value system are compared to the worldview and value system of the United States.

For two countries which share similar geographical circumstances and cultural traditions, one would expect the worldviews and value systems of the two countries to be much more similar than they are. However, not only do Canadians and Americans see the world differently and act in the world differently, but also Canadian culture and American culture are very different when they are compared as wholes.

This is apparent as soon as the historical development and constitutional arrangements of the two countries are examined. Whereas the historical development of the United States has been based on revolution and competition, the historical development of Canada has been based on evolution, compromise and concession. Whereas the Constitution of the United States is based primarily on the principles of life, liberty and the pursuit of happiness, the Constitution of Canada is based largely on peace, order and good government. These differences, which are by no means limited to historical development and constitutional arrangements but extend across many domains and areas of cultural life, betray fundamental differences in the way Canadians and Americans see the world and value things in the world. These differences become clear as soon as Canadians travel abroad. For while many Canadians lament the fact that the differences between the two cultures and their worldviews and value systems are not immediately apparent at home, they are instantly recognized outside of Canada. This is because the differences between the two cultures and their worldviews and value systems are more visible to people living in other cultures and parts of the world, as well as more visible to Canadians when they are outside the country and are travelling abroad.

These differences are worth preserving. Many Canadians originally came to Canada because they were rebelling against worldviews and value systems in existence in other parts of the world and were anxious to participate in the building of a culture which had a different worldview and value system than the one they were leaving. What they have created, over many centuries, is a culture that is peace-loving, co-operative, caring, compassionate and humane, largely because it is based on a very specific way of looking at the world and valuing things in the world. It is a culture worth protecting, preserving and developing in the future because it relates so fundamentally to what Canada and Canadians are all about.

THE CENTRALITY OF CANADIAN CULTURE

> Culture, however we define it, is central to everything we do and think. It is what we do and the reasons why we do it, what we wish and why we imagine it, what we perceive and how we express it, how we live and in what manner we approach death. It is our environment and the patterns of our adaptation to it. It is the world we have created and are still creating; it is the way we see that world and the motives that urge us to change it. It is the way we know ourselves and each other; it is our web of personal relationship; it is the images and abstractions that allow us to live together in communities and nations. It is the element in which we live.
>
> Bernard Ostry[1]

Now that the problem of ascertaining how it is possible to know Canadian culture has been dealt with and a portrait has been created of the country's culture using the insights of Canadian artists, scholars, historians, architects, philosophers and critics as a guide, it is possible to ask how important Canadian culture is in the total scheme of things.

When Canadian culture is defined in holistic terms, it is clear that it should be accorded a central position in the total scheme of things. Indeed, it should be made the centrepiece of Canadian development and dealt with accordingly. This is because the whole *determines* the parts and therefore should take precedence over the parts. Ruth Benedict, the renowned cultural scholar and author of *Patterns of Culture*, explains why this is so necessary:

> The whole determines its parts, not only their relation but their very nature....The whole, as modern science is insisting in many fields, is not merely the sum of all its parts, but the result of a unique arrangement and inter-relation of the parts *that has brought about a new reality.*[2]

---

[1] Bernard Ostry. *The Cultural Connection: An Essay on Culture and Government Policy in Canada.* McClelland & Stewart. Toronto. 1978. p. 1.

[2] Ruth Benedict. *Patterns of Culture.* Routledge and Kegan Paul Ltd. London. 1961. pp. 36 and 33. (emphasis mine).

The implications of this line of argument are clear and unequivocal. No action or activity which is detrimental or inimical to the interests of Canadian culture **as a whole** should be pursued or sanctioned. What this means in practice is that no economic, commercial, financial, social, political, technological, or other action should be taken if it runs counter to the interests of Canadian culture viewed as a total, integrated entity.

Making Canadian culture the centrepiece of Canadian development and placing the country's cultural interests ahead of other interests will not be easy. Not only is Canadian culture not mentioned at all in the British North America Act — unlike many other interests which receive prominent billing — but also there is a penchant in Canada and the world at present to place the interests of the parts ahead of the interests of the whole. This is particularly true for the economy, but it is also true for other interests. Regardless of how important the economy and other interests are, and there is no intention of diminishing or deprecating their importance here, what must be recognized is that economic and other interests are parts of the whole and not the whole itself, and therefore should be accorded a secondary rather than principal priority in the total scheme of things.

Looked at in this way, Canadian culture is concerned with questions and issues of the greatest importance and utmost urgency to Canada and Canadians. How can Canadians evolve a way of life which simultaneously protects the environment and preserves people's jobs and sources of livelihood? How can the country's municipal governments conduct their affairs so that Canadians can profit from decent income, employment, educational, social, recreational and artistic amenities in their own localities and communities? How can the country's provincial and federal governments create the policies, programmes and processes which are necessary to permit Canadians to enjoy a reasonable measure of material comfort, health care, social security and personal and collective fulfilment? How can Canadians organize their affairs so that they live creative, constructive and fulfilling lives, as well as respect the rights, values, traditions and beliefs of others? How can the conflicts and tensions which exist among the various peoples of Canada be resolved?

And how can the country configure its international affairs and trading arrangements so that sovereignty, autonomy and independence are assured in the years and decades ahead? These are the tough, concrete and immensely practical questions with which Canadian culture is concerned — questions which have the greatest significance and utmost relevance to the country and its citizenry.

It is clear from the profound and pressing nature of these questions that the scope and orbit of Canadian culture is immense. Not only does Canadian culture encompass all aspects and manifestations of reality — the negative as well as the positive, the violence, power, oppression and exploitation as well as the ethics and ideals, the hopes and dreams as well as the fears, the theoretical as well as the practical — but also it is concerned with the entire spectrum of pains and pleasures, prejudices and potentialities, and adversities and accomplishments which constitute Canadian development. If Canadians are to be successful in addressing these issues in the future, it will be necessary to accord Canadian culture the highest possible priority in public and private policy and decision-making. Such a priority would make the development of Canadian culture the heart and soul of all Canadian development in the future.

CANADIAN CULTURE: CENTREPIECE OF CANADIAN DEVELOPMENT

Seeing and treating Canadian culture as the centrepiece of Canadian development will necessitate a profound shift in consciousness about the nature, purpose and character of Canadian development. It is a shift not unlike the shift that is required when Canadian culture is conceived and defined as a whole rather than as a part of a whole.

As matters now stand, the Canadian economy is seen and treated as the centrepiece and principal preoccupation of Canadian development. Not only does it receive the lion's share of public and private attention, but also it is generally assumed that as the Canadian economy goes, so goes Canada. While there are some logical and obvious reasons for this, particularly for people living in a northern culture with many survival and security needs to attend to, there are also a number of reasons why it would be inappropriate to perpetuate this practice in the future.[3]

Regardless of how important the economy is to Canada and Canadians, the economy is a part of the whole and not the whole itself. Thus there is the perpetual danger of the tail wagging the dog: economic policies and practices are condoned which are not always in the best interests of Canada and Canadian culture. Nowhere is this more apparent than in the demands the economy is making on the natural environment and people's lives, largely as a result of insensitive or excessive industrial, commercial and consumption practices, the trading away of control over the country's natural resources, and obsession with economic growth. Clearly if constraints are not placed on the economy and certain types of economic and consumer practices — constraints which should be informed and guided by the broader and deeper interests of Canadian culture as a whole — the economy will not serve Canada and Canadians to best advantage in the future. Moreover, it will not be possible to achieve the kind of "sustained" and "sustainable" development which is necessary if survival, well-being and the needs of future generations are to be looked after most effectively in the years and decades ahead.

Regardless of how important the creation of a viable economy is or has been in the thoughts, minds and actions of Canadians, successive generations of Canadians have struggled over the centuries to build a *culture*, not an economy. It is a culture capable of meeting the needs of Canadians for security, survival, sustenance, health, happiness and creative fulfilment in all aspects and dimensions of cultural life. This has always been the main motive behind Canadian development and it would be foolhardy not to recognize it. For this fact is of crucial importance in understanding the past, coming to grips with the present and confronting the future.

---

[3] D. Paul Schafer. "Cultures and Economies: Irresistible Forces Encounter Immovable Objects." *Futures: The Journal of Forecasting, Planning and Policy.* Volume 26, No. 8. October 1994. pp. 830-845.

With this fact clearly in mind, what can be said about Canadian development in the years and decades ahead? Surely this. It is the principal task and fundamental purpose of Canadian development to create a culture which is **comprehensive, coherent, cohesive, humane and contexted properly in the natural and historical environment**.[4]

In order to create a culture which is *comprehensive*, it is necessary to develop *all* the resources of the country and not just economic and technological resources. This includes, besides economic and technological resources, social, political, scientific, artistic, educational, environmental, recreational and spiritual resources. Thanks to the efforts of countless generations of Canadians, many if not most of these resources are already in a high state of development throughout the country at the present time. However, to be fully developed, the country needs not only a well-developed and strong economy, it also needs a well-developed and strong educational system, first-class social programmes, a dynamic and progressive scientific and artistic community, and an enlightened set of environmental and ethical policies.

If Canadian culture should be comprehensive, it should also be *coherent*. Whereas comprehensiveness is achieved by creating a well-rounded and diversified constellation of cultural resources, coherence is achieved by creating a harmonious and synergistic relationship between and among these resources.

Creating a harmonious and synergistic relationship between all the resources which constitute Canadian culture will not be easy. Not only do serious imbalances exist at the present time between some of the most essential resources of the country, such as the imbalance that exists between economic and environmental resources and technological and spiritual resources, but also serious imbalances exist between many of the component parts of Canadian culture. Nowhere is this more apparent than in the imbalance that exists between the material and non-material or quantitative and qualitative dimensions of the country's culture.

---

[4] D. Paul Schafer. *The Challenge of Cultural Development.* World Culture Project. Markham. 1994.

Whereas the material or quantitative dimensions of the country's culture are more developed at present, much more emphasis will have to be placed on the development of the non-material or qualitative dimensions of the country's culture if Canadians are to solve the environmental crisis and the crisis of maldevelopment, or spiritual poverty in the midst of plenty.

If it is necessary to create a culture which is coherent, it is equally necessary to create a culture which is *cohesive*. In fact, this is probably the biggest challenge confronting Canada and Canadians of all. Whereas the country's culture is reasonably comprehensive and coherent, it is still far from being cohesive. Not only have Canadians failed to create "the ties that bind" as an increasing number of authors put it, but also the various geographical, linguistic, ethnic and social divisions that exist through the country threaten to undermine the country as a whole. This makes creating a cohesive culture a fundamental priority for the future. The quintessential role that artists and scholars play in this process cannot be denied. For, as indicated earlier, it is the country's painters, writers, poets, composers, choreographers, singers, dancers, actors, architects, scholars, historians and the like who create the artistic and scholarly works which are needed to bind Canada and Canadians together when other forces are operating to split them apart.

Like the need to develop a cohesive culture, there is also a need to develop a humane culture. Whereas a cohesive culture is as free as possible from divisions and is firmly committed to convergence rather than divergence in its cultural life, a humane culture is as free as possible from human rights abuses and other types of social and human injustices.

It is difficult to assess Canada's record in this most essential area of cultural life. On the one hand, Canada has compiled a very impressive record in terms of reducing or eliminating many types of human rights abuses and other types of social injustices through the passing of the British North America Act, the Charter of Rights and Freedoms, the current policy of pluralism and aggressive human rights legislation. On the other hand, the country still has a long way to go in this area, as the treatment of the native peoples, the internment of the Japanese during World War II and the dealings with various ethnic minorities demonstrate. This makes creation of a humane culture a perpetual preoccupation — a preoccupation which is every bit as important as the other achievements which must be realized if Canada and Canadians are to have a well-rounded and fully-developed cultural life.

It is impossible to have a well-rounded and fully-developed cultural life if the country's culture is not situated properly in the natural and historical environment. For just as Canadian culture provides the context within which the component parts of the country's culture are located, so, as indicated earlier, the natural and historical environment provides the context within which Canadian culture as a whole is situated.

Properly situating Canadian culture in the natural and historical environment may prove to be the most difficult challenge confronting Canadians and Canadian development of all. Situating Canadian culture properly in the *natural* environment will not only require altered consumption practices and life-style changes — consumption practices and life-style changes which make fewer demands on the resources of nature and are much more in keeping with the country's fragile eco-system. It will also require a wholesale transformation in the way Canadians perceive the natural environment and interact with it in the future. Despite the difficulties involved in this, situating Canadian culture properly in the *historical* environment may prove to be even more difficult. It will require a re-writing of Canadian history along more authentic and accurate lines — lines which recognize and respect the seminal contributions that all the various peoples of Canada have made and continue to make to the development of Canada and Canadian culture. For only in this way will it be possible to correct many of the historical injustices and inaccuracies which have long smouldered in the side of Canadian history when it is viewed from a cultural or holistic perspective.

If Canadian culture is to be contexted properly in the natural and historical environment and is to be comprehensive, coherent, cohesive and humane as well, Canadians will have to exercise a great deal of control over the development of their culture and all aspects of cultural life. Not only will they have to possess the autonomy and independence which is necessary to determine how they would like the component parts of their culture to be organized and ordered, but also they will have to be able to decide for themselves how they would like their culture to evolve and develop as an integrated and organic whole. For only in this way will it be possible to create a culture which meets the needs of Canadians for security, survival and well-being, is finely tuned to Canada's specific situation and particular circumstances, and is properly contexted in space and time.

FOUR CRUCIAL CULTURAL RELATIONSHIPS

If Canadian culture is to be seen and treated as the centrepiece of Canadian development in the future, much more attention will have to be given to cultural relationships in general and strategic cultural relationships in particular. Four specific cultural relationships have been selected for analysis here because they are destined to have a fundamental bearing on Canadian development and Canadian culture in the future. These four relationships are: the relationship between Canadian culture and the Canadian economy; the relationship between Canadian culture and Canadian politics; the relationship between Canadian culture and Canadian ethics; and viewed from a much larger perspective, the relationship between Canadian culture and the natural and historical environment. While these are not the only relationships with which Canadian culture and Canadian development are concerned, they are of crucial importance to Canada and Canadians in the future.

No relationship is more difficult to pin down or come to grips with than the relationship between Canadian culture and the Canadian economy. As indicated earlier, whereas Canadian culture has been seen and treated in the past and is seen and treated at present as a component part of the Canadian economy, it is more appropriate to see and treat the Canadian economy as a component part of Canadian culture in the future.

Treating the Canadian economy as a component part of Canadian culture means accepting the fact that the country's culture provides the context or container within which the Canadian economy is situated and developed. This means bringing broader and deeper forces to bear on the development of the Canadian economy, rather than allowing the Canadian economy to function as an independent force or autonomous entity in its own right.

Many practical advantages could accrue from contexting the Canadian economy properly in the larger framework of Canadian culture. In the first place, it would be possible to bring the more specific goals and objectives of the Canadian economy — consumption, investment, productivity, efficiency, employment, growth and profits — into line with the more general goals and objectives of Canadian culture — excellence, creativity, love of knowledge, wisdom and beauty, co-operation, sharing, caring, promotion of cultural identity, respect for cultural diversity and safe-guarding of the cultural heritage.[5] In the second place, it would be possible to reduce the demands that the Canadian economy make on the natural environment and the resources of nature because much more emphasis would be placed on the qualitative as opposed to the quantitative side of Canadian development and hence on activities like the arts, education, learning, social interaction, spiritual fulfilment, conservation and permanence which tend to conserve rather than consume natural resources. Finally, it would make it possible to rejuvenate, revitalize and humanize the Canadian economy because a much higher priority would be placed on creativity, diversity, innovation and the human factor in development than on uniformity, conformity, standardization, competition and the technological factor in development.[6]

Rejuvenation, revitalization and humanization of the Canadian economy are of vital importance to the country and its citizenry in the future. Rejuvenation and revitalization is necessary in order to shake the

---

[5] Most of these goals and objectives are firmly entrenched in the principles and practices of Canada's cultural agencies and the works of Canadian and international cultural scholars.

[6] Recreating the development process so that it meets the needs and concerns of people has been a major concern of UNESCO and other cultural agencies for more than a decade. See, for example, *Rethinking Development: World Decade for Cultural Development 1988-1997*. UNESCO. Paris. 1994.

economy out of its lethargy and ensure that it is capable of meeting the demands that Canadians place on it for a decent standard of living as well as well-developed social programmes, educational and scientific endeavours and artistic amenities. And humanization is necessary in order to ensure that economic interests do not get too divorced from human needs and the concerns of Canadians as citizens. Viewed from this perspective, it is clear where the solution to the current economic malaise lies. It lies in creativity, co-operation, collaboration, caring, and income, employment, job and resource sharing. For this is what re-asserting the human factor in development and economic activity is all about.

If it is essential to deal with the complex relationship between Canadian culture and the Canadian economy, it is equally essential to deal with the complex relationship between Canadian culture and Canadian politics.

Just as the Canadian economy should be contexted within Canadian culture if it is to develop and function properly, so Canadian politics should be contexted in Canadian culture if the country's political systems and practices are to develop and function properly.

Given this fundamental requirement, what can be said about the relationship between Canadian culture and Canadian politics? Surely this. *It is the first and foremost responsibility Canada's federal, provincial and municipal governments in general, and politicians and civil servants in particular, to develop Canadian culture.* In order to achieve this, governments, politicians and civil servants at all levels will have to abandon their penchant for thinking about Canadian culture in narrow and specialized terms and start thinking about Canadian culture as the very essence and raison d'être of their existence.

Realization of this state of affairs will require a fundamental transformation in political and governmental priorities, procedures, structures, models, policies, programmes and practices. Parliaments and cabinets will have to devote much more time and attention to discussing and debating the development of Canadian culture; cultural departments and agencies will have to become the principal departments and agencies in government; cultural models will have to replace economic models as the primary vehicles for political and governmental decision-making; and cultural policy will have to be accorded the highest possible priority in public policy. Without this, Canadian culture and Canadian development will be seriously short-changed and impeded in the future.

As it is visualized here, there is an intimate relationship and natural affinity between Canadian culture and Canadian politics. The reason for this is clear. Both Canadian culture and Canadian politics are concerned with the whole, and therefore with asserting the interests of the whole over the interests of the parts. As such, the mandate of both Canadian politics and Canadian culture is to ensure that Canada's cultural whole is structured and ordered properly and there is a harmonious and synergistic relationship between and among the component parts of this whole.

Despite the intimate relationship and natural affinity between Canadian culture and Canadian politics, there will be times when these two forces will be in conflict. Take the conflict that exists between unity and identity as one illustration of this. Northrop Frye drew attention to the potential conflict between politics and culture when he talked about the tension that exists between unity and identity and the dangers that are inherent in it:

> Assimilating identity to unity produces the empty gestures of cultural nationalism; assimilating unity to identity produces the kind of provincial isolation which is now called separatism.[7]

While the tension between unity and identity is the most conspicuous type of conflict that exists between Canadian culture and Canadian politics, it is not the only type of conflict which exists. Indeed,

---

[7] Northrop Frye. *The Bush Garden: Essays on the Canadian Imagination.* Anansi. 1971. pp. iii .

there is a whole series of actual and potential conflict points between Canadian culture and Canadian politics.

In general, Canadian politics is concerned with peace, order, justice, equality, security and good government. Canadian culture is concerned with excellence, creativity, beauty, freedom of expression and participation. Thus the potential for conflict is always present. The cultural community may be concerned with creativity at the very moment this is inimical to order. Since creativity often involves destruction before construction — old structures must be torn down before new ones can be created — this may be unpalatable or unacceptable to politicians and governments. Or to cite another example, citizens may feel the need for freedom of expression at the very time politicians and governments may feel this is inimical to peace and security. Whereas citizens may feel that unrestrained expression and free flow of information and ideas is the best way to achieve freedom and truth, politicians and governments may feel that censorship is the best way to maintain peace and security.

It is impossible to determine how specific conflicts like these should be resolved since each will depend on the specific situation and circumstances at the time and should be judged on its own merits. In general, however, conflicts like these should always be resolved in a manner that is consistent with the interests of the "cultural whole." More often than not, this means that they should be resolved in the interests of culture. For history confirms the fact that countries which suppress creativity, freedom and truth sooner or later pay a severe price.

If the relationship between Canadian culture and Canadian politics is a complex and difficult one, so to is the relationship between Canadian culture and Canadian ethics. In fact, it is probably even more complex and difficult because it is impossible to examine and deal with the relationship between Canadian culture and Canadian ethics without raising the related problem of religion and morality.

There is no question that ethical issues and concerns are gaining increased prominence in Canadian society today. On the one hand, governments and political institutions are experiencing more and more pressure to institute ethical codes to govern their behaviour and the behaviour of their members. On the other hand, more and more questions are being raised about the need to establish ethical standards in business and society generally — standards which determine how companies, commercial establishments and people relate to one another and the public at large.

What accounts for the rapidly-escalating interest in ethical issues and concerns throughout Canada? Primarily it is due to the realization that ethical principles and practices constitute a quintessential dimension of Canadian cultural life. Although much more needs to be known about the reason for cultural decline and collapse, it is clear that cultures decline and collapse for two principal reasons. The first has to do with the failure of cultures to give sufficient consideration to the natural environment and the conservation of natural resources. The second has to do with the progressive decay of the moral and ethical fibre of cultures. This makes ethical issues and concerns a consideration of key importance to the development and maturation of any culture.

In most cases, it is religion which provides the moral and ethical content for cultures. With the separation of church and state, the relegation of religion to the private sector and the declining interest in religion in many parts of the world, moral and ethical issues and concerns are being pushed farther and farther into the background in many cultures. Nevertheless, they continue to fester away in the side of cultures and call out for confrontation and reconciliation.

Such is the situation that Canada, Canadians and Canadian culture appear to be confronted with at the present time. With the separation of the secular from the sacred and the "privatization" of religion, Canada and Canadians find themselves in need of a "secular ethical code" which can govern relationships between public and private institutions and the Canadian population at large. Such a code should be based on the commonly-accepted ethical principles and practices found in the majority and diversity of religions prevalent in Canada at the present time: caring for fellow human beings; resource sharing; equality; differentiation between right and wrong; and respect for the natural environment and the needs of other species and future generations. The educational system and the family, however they are defined, should provide the principal conduits for this ethical code, not in the sacred sense of an ethical code that is wrapped in the traditional trappings of religion, but rather in the secular sense of an ethical code that is properly contexted in Canadian culture as a whole.

Just as it is necessary to understand the complex relationship that exists between Canadian culture and Canadian ethics, so it is necessary to understand the complex relationship that exists between Canadian culture and the natural and historical environment. As indicated earlier, just as Canadian culture provides the context or container within which the Canadian economy, Canadian politics and Canadian ethics are situated, so the natural and historical environment provides the context or container within which Canadian culture is located.

Since the importance of situating Canadian culture in the larger natural and historical environment has already been dealt with at some length, it remains to deal with its essence.

From a purely factual and technical point of view, coming to grips with the relationship between Canadian culture and the natural and historical environment means recognizing the way in which Canadian culture has evolved historically and organically in space and time.

In a spatial sense, this means recognizing the progressive evolution of the country's culture in geographical and physical terms, not only from one end of Canada to the other but in other parts of the world as well. On the one hand, this involves broadening and deepening understanding and awareness of the way the environment has provided nourishment and sustenance to the Canadian population. On the other hand, it means broadening and deepening consciousness of the carrying capacity of the natural environment and the various constraints and limitations that should be placed on Canadians' demands on it.

If it is imperative to deal with Canadian culture in a spatial sense, it is even more imperative to deal with it in a temporal sense. For contrary to popular opinion and contemporary belief, Canadian culture is centuries old. For thousands of years prior to the arrival of the Europeans on the scene, the Indians and Inuit were busy establishing the foundations of Canadian culture and planting their roots firmly in Canadian soil. And they did so in exactly the same manner as the Europeans did centuries later, namely by fanning out across the great Dominion of the North and establishing pockets of population and settlements whenever and wherever geographical conditions and environmental circumstances proved feasible.

There can be no "authentic" development of Canadian culture until the original roots, pioneering achievements and seminal contributions of the native peoples are recognized and given their due in the country's history books, legal arrangements and constitutional accords. Not only does the quest for truth demand it, but also the dictates of justice compel it. Regardless of how crucial a role the French, the English and other groups played in bringing Canada into existence in a legal, constitutional and political sense — and there is no intention of diminishing or undermining these contributions here — it was the Indian and Inuit peoples of Canada who were the founding peoples of Canada in a cultural sense.

The fact that Canada possesses cultural roots and traditions which stretch back to the earliest origins of Indian and Inuit life in Canada means that the country possesses a cultural history which is thousands of years old. It is a history which has been punctuated by numerous challenges and achievements as well as some fundamental turning points, such as the role the native peoples played at the *genesis* of Canadian cultural development, the arrival of the first Europeans, the contributions of the English, the French and other ethnic groups to the "opening up" of Canada and indeed the whole North American continent, the creation of the country as a political and geographical entity, and the pluralistic and multicultural reality of the country so conspicuous today. To settle for any other view of Canadian culture, such as Canada was a cultural "wasteland" prior to the twentieth century, Canada's cultural development started with the arrival of the first Europeans, or Canadian culture is a post World War II phenomenon, is to settle for a view of the country's culture and its development which is not consistent with the facts and the history of the matter.

If Canadians should be acting to situate Canadian culture properly in the natural and historical environment in a purely factual and technical sense, they should also be acting to situate the country's culture properly in the natural and historical environment in a deeper and more profound spiritual sense. Whereas the former involves changes in the country's history books, legal enactments and constitutional arrangements, the latter involves changes in the hearts, minds, souls and spirits of Canadians.

In spiritual terms, coming to grip with the relationship between Canadian culture and the natural and historical environment means recognizing the more fundamental cosmological, mythological, philosophical, ontological, theological, and metaphysical forces which connect Canadians to their history and the land. On the one hand, this means seeing and treating the natural environment as a unique and precious spiritual gift — a gift that requires a great deal of reverence and humility on the part of its recipients. Such a realization goes far beyond the realization that the natural environment provides the material nourishment and sustenance which is necessary to sustain life to include a sense of awe, wonder and gratitude for the majesty and grandeur of nature and the existence of other species. On the other hand, it means accepting the fact that the genesis and roots of Canadian culture are aboriginal rather than European, with all this entails in terms of the symbolism attached to genesis and roots for everything that comes thereafter. Recognition of this fact should cause Canadians to see the native peoples in a new light, as well as to re-create their culture and relationship with the natural and historical environment in such a way that it is more consistent and in keeping with aboriginal worldviews, values, perceptions and beliefs.

This completes the probe of four strategic relationships which lie at the heart and soul of Canadian culture and Canadian development. While these are not the only relationships with which Canadian culture and Canadian development are concerned, they demonstrate the crucial role that relationships in general, and context and contexting in particular, play in influencing all aspects and dimensions of Canadian life.

THE DEVELOPMENT OF CANADIAN CULTURE

> Development is not merely an economic and political concept; it is more fundamentally a process of culture and civilization.
>
> Report of the Scheveningen Symposium[1]

Now that the centrality of Canadian culture has been addressed, it is possible to proceed to the development of Canadian culture. How is the country's culture developed and what are the most important factors in this development?

For many Canadians, the starting point for the development of Canadian culture lies in building up the cultural resources of the country: commercial and industrial establishments, manufacturing ventures, government departments and agencies, social welfare groups, arts organizations, communications networks, and the like. For others, it lies in the creation of cultural opportunities: employment and income possibilities, investment activities, recreational amenities, educational activities and health care programmes. However much cultural resources need building up and cultural opportunities require activation, there really is only one place for Canadian cultural development to start and that is with people. It is people who should constitute the springboard or point of departure for development of the country's culture.

THE IMPORTANCE OF PEOPLE

Why are people the most important factor in Canadian cultural development? Without people, the efforts of cultural institutions are irrelevant since there is no one to appreciate their work and benefit from their efforts. In addition, people constitute the most basic ingredient of

---

[1] *The Scheveningen Report: Towards a New International Development Strategy.* Scheveningen Symposium. 25-28 July, 1979. International Foundation for Development Alternatives. Nyon. 1979. p.7.

cultural development of all, and therefore the point of departure for any meaningful penetration into the cultural life of a country. Moreover, it is people, taken individually and collectively, who determine the character of cultural development, and therefore the various patterns, rhythms and themes which characterize this development. Finally, and perhaps most importantly of all, it is people who give cultural development a human and humane face. Without this, cultural development is doomed to failure, regardless of how it is defined and executed.

Given the importance of people to Canadian cultural development, it is necessary to delve deeply into the cultural requirements of Canadians. What are the cultural needs of Canadians? Does an adequate stock of cultural resources and opportunities exist to meet these needs? Can Canadians participate fully and effectively in the cultural life of the community, the region, the province and the country as a whole? Are Canadians actively engaged in the various plans, policies and programmes which shape their lives? Do Canadians have the freedom, as well as the means, to create alternative forms of cultural expression to those which are already in existence? These are crucial questions for Canadian culture in general and Canadian development in particular.

In attempting to address these questions and work out suitable answers to them, Canadians enter into a complex relationship with their culture and the state. On the one hand, there are certain cultural rights to be enjoyed as a result of being a Canadian and a citizen of Canada. On the other hand, there are certain cultural responsibilities to execute in return.

Of the two, it is cultural responsibilities which deserve the greatest attention. This is because so much attention has been focused on cultural rights over the last four or five decades that the very idea of cultural responsibilities pales by comparison. And yet, of the two, it is cultural responsibilities that are the most important at this particular juncture in the cultural development of the country.

Of what do Canadians' cultural responsibilities consist? Surely they consist of a responsibility to acquire the skills and abilities which are necessary to participate actively in the cultural life of the community and the country, to acquire a reasonable knowledge and understanding of the historical and contemporary development of the country's culture, to engage fully in programming, policy and decision-making activities, and to respect the values, traditions and beliefs of others. While these are not the only cultural responsibilities of Canadians, adherence to them should ensure that Canadians are meeting the demands and dictates of citizenship in a responsible and effective manner.

While far too little attention has been focused on cultural responsibilities over the last three or four decades, the same cannot be said for cultural rights. In fact, most governments and international organizations have focused primarily on the identification and assertion of cultural rights over the last half century. As a result, at the international level, there has been the signing of such proclamations as the Universal Declaration of Human Rights which recognizes the importance of respecting and responding to the cultural needs of people. Here at home, there has been the signing of the Charter of Rights and Freedoms, the creation of human rights commissions and equity legislation concerned with recognizing and protecting the cultural rights of Canadians. While much work remains to be done in this area, clearly developments to date represent a valuable step in the right direction.

As they are visualized and articulated here, the cultural rights of Canadians are not limited to the right to work, the right to education, the right to a reasonable standard of living and the right to freedom of expression, although this is very much part of it. More fundamentally, a whole spectrum of rights is involved, from economic, educational, political and legal rights to social, spiritual, artistic and scientific rights. While there is no guarantee that these rights can always be realized, particularly the ones that have to do with the state of the economy and maintenance of a high standard of living, every effort should be made to ensure that as many of these rights are protected and fulfilled as possible.

It is clear from this that Canadian citizenship is a dynamic rather than a static affair. It is not something that is acquired at birth or conferred on people after the elapse of a certain period of time or the memorization of a specified amount of data, but something that is continuously expanding and constantly being upgraded and extended. Not only are there countless cultural rights to be identified and fought for, but also there are specific cultural responsibilities to be addressed and executed in return. This means that much more energy and effort will have to go into the understanding, practice and fulfilment of Canadian citizenship in the future.

Visualized in this way, there is an intimate bond between Canadians as citizens on the one hand and the development of Canadian culture on the other hand. Surely Canadian cultural development is every citizen's business. Not only do all Canadians have a fundamental role to play in it, but all Canadians have a valuable and necessary contribution to make to it. This contribution may be large or small, local or national, visible or invisible, but it is always there. This is what makes it possible to talk about "the human dimension" of Canadian cultural development, as well as to recognize that Canadians as people and as citizens are at the very heart and soul of the country's cultural life.

THE SIGNIFICANCE OF EDUCATION

It is impossible to have high quality Canadian citizenship and give Canadian cultural development a human and humane face without first-class education. With first-class education, Canadians, Canadian citizenship and Canadian culture are bound to flourish. Without it, they are certain to languish.

As it is envisaged here, education goes far beyond preparation for a specific job or training for a particular profession. It is education that embraces all aspects of the human condition, from the spiritual, ethical, environmental, artistic and social to the economic, political, scientific and technological. Moreover, it encompasses all aspects and dimensions of the learning process, from formal, informal, adult and continuing education to life-long learning. It is education in the most comprehensive and complete sense of the term.

Consistent with the holistic definition of Canadian culture set out earlier, Canadian education should be centred on the development of "the whole person." Such a person should possess the specific skills and abilities which are necessary to secure a job and earn a livelihood, but also to derive maximum fulfilment and satisfaction from all aspects of the country's cultural life. In order to achieve this, it is not only essential to develop the intellectual, emotional, physical, spiritual, aesthetic and technical capabilities of the individual, it is also essential to realize a harmonious and synergistic relationship among them.

It is difficult to see how education of the whole person can be achieved in Canada without a fundamental education in the arts. As indicated earlier, the arts not only provide the key to knowledge, experience and understanding of Canadian culture through familiarity with symbols, metaphors, myths, stories and allegories which stand for the whole. They also provide the key to developing all aspects and dimensions of the Canadian personality. For unlike many other disciplines which focus on the development of one or two aspects or dimensions of the Canadian personality, the arts deal with all the cognitive, affective, physical, spiritual, perceptual and aesthetic capabilities of the Canadian personality in concert.

There is an additional reason why the arts should be given a high priority in Canada's educational system. Given the nature of contemporary economic and technological development, the high rate of occupational turnover and the dynamic character of modern society, Canadians will have to develop all their creative abilities to the utmost if they are to survive in a rapidly-changing and complex world. More than any other discipline, it is the arts which possess the ability to unlock the secrets and innate creativity of Canadians. Through a solid and comprehensive education in the arts, Canadians will be able to develop their creative potential to the fullest extent, as well as to apply it to each and every aspect of the country's economic, commercial, political, social and environmental life. It matters little whether Canadians are working in the primary, secondary or tertiary sectors of society, or are engaged in any other type of activity or endeavour. What matters most is that they are able to express their creativity in inventive and original ways and discover innovative solutions to problems and challenges.

Armed with a solid and comprehensive education in the arts, Canadians should be in an ideal position to acquire the education they need in other fields and disciplines to function effectively in Canadian society and participate fully in the country's cultural life. Herein lies the ultimate litmus test for Canadian education. Has the quality and character of the education of Canadians been such that they are able to play a responsible role in the cultural life of the community, the province and the country, as well as assume the duties and responsibilities of Canadian citizenship? Can Canadians make original and meaningful contributions to the country's cultural development? Answers to these questions will determine in large measure whether Canadian education is filling the mandate that is visualized for it here.

It is impossible for Canadians to play a responsible role in Canadian cultural development and make original and meaningful contributions to the country's cultural life without progressively broadening and deepening their knowledge and understanding of Canadian culture. Herein lies one of the greatest challenges of Canadian education of all. At the present time, many Canadians lack a well-rounded knowledge and understanding of the evolution, historical development, contemporary reality and character of Canadian culture. As a result, they lack the bonds and links which are necessary to tie the country and its citizenry together.

In order to rectify this, much more time and energy will have to be devoted to learning about all aspects and dimensions of Canadian culture in the future. This includes, among countless other things, exposure to and awareness of the cultural accomplishments of the Indians and Inuit, the evolution of the country's culture century by century and province by province, the contributions of Canadians to the cultural heritage of humankind,[2] the works of the country's artists, scientists and scholars, and the achievements of the nation's many ethnic communities and minority groups. This latter dimension is particularly important in view of the multicultural character of the Canadian population and the need to cultivate respect for the rights, traditions and values of others in an increasingly multiracial and multidimensional world.

THE DEMOCRATIZATION OF CULTURAL RESOURCES

It is fitting that the democratization of cultural resources should follow the significance of education and the importance of people. For people and education, particularly as they relate to questions of citizenship, cultural rights and responsibilities and preparation for participation in cultural life, are deeply rooted in the democratization of cultural resources.

In a democratic country like Canada, the democratization of cultural resources has two principal meanings. On the one hand, it means access to existing resources. On the other hand, it means creation of new resources.

Access to existing resources is achieved by eliminating or reducing as many barriers to entry as possible. These barriers may be technical, mechanical, informational, financial, economic, social, educational, linguistic, geographical, or religious. Some of these barriers may be eliminated or reduced by lowering the cost of admission, raising the standard of living, or increasing the level and quality of education. Others, however, may prove more difficult to deal with, such as barriers that are caused by religious sanctions, prejudice, racism, social conventions and stereotyping.

While Canada's record in dealing with these barriers is far from perfect and requires improvement, much has been achieved in terms of eliminating or reducing barriers to entry over the last four decades as a

---

2 See, for example, J.J. Brown. *Ideas in Exile: A History of Canadian Inventions.* McClelland & Stewart. Toronto. 1967.

result of human rights legislation and commissions, the creation of race relations agencies, and the like. Thanks to efforts like these in neighbourhoods, communities, regions and provinces all across the country, Canadians now have more access to the myriad cultural resources which exist throughout the country than at any other time in the nation's history.

While access to existing cultural resources is a goal worthy of pursuit, so is the creation of *new* cultural resources. Whenever existing resources do not meet people's needs or fill the bill, Canadians should have opportunities to create alternative resources for themselves.

Opening up opportunities for Canadians to create alternative cultural resources is a difficult matter. Not only does the lion's share of public and private funding go to the promotion and distribution of existing resources, but also providing citizens with public and private funds to create resources themselves requires a great deal of trust, courage, and the willingness to take risk on the part of governments, corporations, foundations and other funding agencies.

But there are precedents. One such precedent is the Opportunities for Youth and Local Initiatives programmes which were created in the nineteen-seventies by the federal government to combat high levels of unemployment. Rather than funding existing activities, Canadians were provided with funds to create alternative resources of their own choosing. The results were phenomenal, thereby suggesting that programmes like these could serve as models for similar undertakings in an era of high unemployment and growing part-time employment. Not only were a significant number of the projects undertaken through Opportunities for Youth and the Local Initiatives Programme "cultural" in nature — somewhere between thirty and fifty percent based on the "official definition of Canadian culture" — but also an overwhelming number of the projects were "Canadian" in the sense that they were concerned with Canadian issues, content and problems. Moreover, they led to the creation of many Canadian arts organizations, such as theatre companies and artist-run galleries, which are highly active and stable today and occupy a fundamental place in Canada's overall cultural landscape.[3] Examples like these, which appear all too infrequently in the history of Canadian government, corporate and foundation activity, suggest that the cause of democratization could be served very well in the future by dramatic increases in the opportunities available to Canadians to create alternative cultural resources for themselves.

THE DECENTRALIZATION OF CULTURAL ACTIVITIES

It is a well-known fact that there is constant pressure for decentralization in Canada. The provincial governments are constantly pressing the federal government for more control, power and authority over their administrative, financial, fiscal, legal and constitutional affairs, just as regional and municipal governments are constantly pressing provincial governments for similar powers and prerogatives.

As indicated earlier, the pressure for decentralization is understandable in a country as large, diversified and sparsely-populated as Canada. While many are concerned about the erosion of federal power and the need to maintain a strong federal government in order to keep the country together, it seems likely that increased decentralization will be necessary in the future to deal with the forces of globalization and do justice to the dictates and demands of the country's cultural life.

As far as the forces of globalization are concerned, many Canadians are coming to the conclusion that it is the quality of life in their communities, neighbourhoods and municipalities that is the decisive factor in life. If Canadian communities, neighbourhoods and municipalities lack a balanced and diversified array of cultural resources and reasonable access to these resources, no amount of globalization, industrial growth, technological change, trade agreements, or international trade will make up the difference. This is manifesting itself in the creation of a number of countervailing measures aimed at counteracting globalization, the

---

[3] D. Paul Schafer and André Fortier. *Review of Federal Policies for the Arts in Canada (1944-1988)*. Canadian Conference of the Arts. Ottawa. 1989. p. 31.

emergence of larger and larger trading blocks and the appearance of political and economic superstates. Most of these movements are designed to restore people's sense of community, solidarity and control over the decision-making processes affecting their lives.

As far as the dictates and demands of the country's cultural life are concerned, decentralization is necessary because Canadian cultural development — like all cultural development — is first and foremost a grassroots affair. Northrop Frye frequently made this point in talking about the differences between cultural development and economic and political development. Whereas economic and political development are centralized in nature and national and international in scope according to Frye, cultural development is decentralized in nature and local and community in character.[4] Augustin Girard, the noted French authority on cultural development, made this same point when he said, "the decentralization of activities...is at once the first step in the direction of cultural democracy and, at the same time, essential to cultural creativity, vitality and freedom. Thus decentralization is necessarily the guiding principle of cultural democracy."[5]

If decentralization is such a crucial part of Canadian cultural development, it is important to ask how well-equipped Canada's communities and municipalities are to cope with the needs of decentralization. Not particularly well by all accounts. Most Canadian communities and municipalities lack the fiscal and financial resources, constitutional powers and institutional infrastructures and mechanisms to deal effectively with the demands and dictates of decentralization. The implications of this are clear and unequivocal: more and more cracks, fissures, tensions and pressures will open up in Canada's communities and municipalities in the future if counteracting developments are not taken

[4] See Northrop Frye. The *Bush Garden: Essays in the Canadian Imagination*. Anansi. Toronto 1971. Also see, Northrop Frye, *Divisions on a Ground: Essays on Canadian Culture*. Edited with a preface by James Polk. Anansi. Toronto. 1982.

[5] Augustin Girard. *Cultural Development: Experience and Policies*. UNESCO Paris. 1972. p. 137. Also see, École des Hautes Études Commerciales. Chaire de Gestion des Arts. *Décentralisation, régionalisation et action culturelle municipale*. Actes du Colloque. Montréal 12-14, November 1992. École des Hautes Études Commerciales. Montréal. 1992.

to prevent it. As this happens, Canadians will probably progressively withdraw from active participation in local life, thereby abandoning their communities and municipalities and surrendering control over decision-making processes to developers, professionals, planners and politicians who may have other interests and motives at heart.

What seems to be at the crux of these matters is the growing fragmentation, compartmentalization and marginalization of Canada's communities and municipalities. With no cultural bonds to bind them together and give them a sense of identity and solidarity, except perhaps for television sets and VCRs, an increasing number of Canadian communities and municipalities are in danger of becoming "callous and impersonal collectivities." Hence the necessity for community and municipal cultural development. Through its ability to treat communities and municipalities as "wholes" and create the social, aesthetic and human bonds which are necessary to keep people together when other forces are operating to split them apart,[6] community and municipal cultural development is able to provide cohesion, solidarity, continuity, and most of all, pride of place.

PATTERNS OF CANADIAN CULTURAL DEVELOPMENT

It is impossible to deal with the question of decentralization of cultural activities and democratization of cultural resources without raising the related question of patterns of cultural development. How democratized, decentralized, centralized, authoritarian, fundamental, or superficial should Canada's pattern of cultural development be? More importantly, what pattern of cultural development is most appropriate for the country and its citizenry at this juncture in the country's history?

In general, it is possible to identify three patterns of cultural development which have the greatest relevance to Canada and Canadians in

---

6 D. Paul Schafer. "Municipalities and Regions: Powerful Forces in a Dynamic World." in *Décentralisation, régionalisation et action culturelle municipale.* ibid. p. 315-329.

the present and the future. These three patterns are the imitative pattern, the imposed pattern and the indigenous pattern.

The imitative pattern traces out the most familiar design. It is based on imitating the worldviews, values, patterns and behavioural characteristics of other countries, particularly Western European countries and the United States. Many would contend that this pattern best depicts the Canadian situation at present. As indicated earlier, not only have Canadians been strongly influenced by the worldviews, outlooks, values, patterns, lifestyles and behavioural characteristics of Western European countries and the United States, but also there appears to be every likelihood of this increasing in the future.

What seems most likely if this pattern is embraced more fully by Canadians in the future is progressive westernization and Americanization of Canadian culture. Through vehicles like the North American Free Trade Agreement and American domination and control of the international modes and instruments of communication in general and Canada's modes of communication in particular, there is a very real possibility that Canadian culture and American culture will be indistinguishable from one another within two or three generations if the imitative pattern is allowed to gain a stranglehold on Canadian culture in the future.

If the imitative pattern is a distinct possibility, so is the imposed pattern. In many ways, it is a more aggravated and extreme form of the imitative pattern. In this case, however, Canadians do not imitate the worldviews, values, patterns, lifestyles and behavioural characteristics of Americans and the western world generally. Rather, they have them imposed on them.

The process whereby this could be achieved is clear. As authors like George Grant and others have pointed out,[7] it has its origins in continentalism and economic and technological integration. While such a

---

[7] George Grant. *Lament for a Nation: The Defeat of Canadian Nationalism.* McClelland & Stewart. Toronto. 1965.

process has been going on for some time, it took a further and more pronounced step in this direction with the signing of the North American Free Trade Agreement. It could eventually culminate with political integration and full Canadian absorption into the United States. Once economic and technological integration were achieved, political and full cultural integration could easily follow. Increasingly, decisions affecting the cultural welfare and well-being of Canada and Canadians would be made south of the border and imposed on Canada and Canadians with or without their approval and consent.

These developments could easily be aggravated or accelerated if Quebec separates from Canada. With Canada broken into a number of distinct parts — the Atlantic region, Ontario, the West, British Columbia and the Northwest Territories — it would not be difficult for the United States to absorb these parts as separate states rather than as a single state. But the outcome would be the same. Slowly but surely, the American way of life would be imposed on the Canadian way of life, as worldviews, values, lifestyles, patterns and modes of behaviour in the hinterland would give way to those of the centre, such as has occurred in many parts of the world and in many periods of history when the pattern of cultural development of one country has been imposed on another country.

Of the three patterns of cultural development, the indigenous pattern is the most difficult to achieve. Rather than acquiescing to the pattern of cultural development prevalent in another country or part of the world, either by imitation or imposition, the indigenous pattern involves pursuing a way of life which evolves naturally and organically out of the roots, soil and traditions of a country's own cultural experiences and circumstances.

Adoption of the indigenous pattern of cultural development means accepting the fact that there is a continuous line of Canadian cultural development stretching back over thousands of years. Given the importance of origins and roots for everything that comes thereafter, it is important to point out that the roots and origins of Canadian culture are Indian and Inuit rather than European. Viewed from this perspective, there is much to be learned from the Indians and Inuit that is germane to Canadian cultural development in the future, particularly as it relates to spirituality, love of nature, respect for ancestors, elders and other species, and living in harmony with the natural environment.

In much the same way that it is imperative to recognize and draw fully on the contributions of the Indians and Inuit if the indigenous pattern of Canadian cultural development is to be achieved, so it is necessary to recognize and draw on the seminal contributions of francophone Canadians. What is too seldom recognized and given its due is the fact that francophone Canadians have made and continue to make vital contributions to Canadian cultural development when it is looked at from an indigenous point of view. Not only was their presence and perseverance instrumental in opening up the entire land mass of North America, thereby making settlement and penetration into the interior of the continent possible, but also francophone Canadians have made countless contributions to Canadian cultural development ever since. In so doing, they have established themselves at the cutting edge of the country's cultural development. Is it any wonder that they are anxious to preserve their culture and maintain control over it?

As the examples of the Indians and Inuit and francophone Canadians illustrate only too well, indigenous Canadian cultural development means digging deeply into the soil, roots and traditions of the country's own cultural development over the centuries and recognizing those cultural challenges, hardships, difficulties and achievements which are unique to Canada and Canadians. And it means something else. It means making hard choices and unpopular decisions about cultural development in the years and decades ahead. On the one hand, this may mean recognizing the seminal contributions of particular groups of Canadians and minority groups which may not be popular with all Canadians. On the other hand, it may mean accepting the fact that Canadians may experience a lower rather than a higher standard of *material* living in the future. For many decisions which are consistent with the cultural needs of the country and Canadian culture as a whole — such as living in harmony with the natural environment and putting more emphasis on the qualitative as opposed to the quantitative side of Canadian cultural development — involve ways of life which conserve rather than consume resources and reduce rather than increase the *material* output of Canadians.

Of all the commitments which are needed to achieve indigenous cultural development, none may be more important than the commitment that is needed to bind the country together in a comprehensive cultural sense. As indicated earlier, this cannot be achieved without much more effective use of the works of Canadian artists and scholars as well as increased control over the country's "cultural and communications industries." Since artists and scholars create the bonds that are necessary to keep the country together when other forces are operating to split it apart, nothing less than a dramatic increase in *indigenous* artistic and scholarly activity will suffice to keep the country together in a total cultural sense. This activity must be matched, if not surpassed, by actions to ensure that the country's cultural and communications industries — radio, television, film publishing, video, satellites, information highways, computers and the like — are firmly in Canadian hands and a reasonable portion of media programming is domestic rather than foreign. Anything less than this will result in the imitative or imposed rather than indigenous pattern of cultural development.

Looked at from this vantage point, it is clear where the main challenge of Canadian cultural development lies in the future. It lies in creating a "shared Canadian culture." While Canadians have been successful in creating a culture which is dynamic, distinctive, responsive and unique, they have yet to create a culture which is shaped, shared, embraced, experienced and engaged in by all Canadians.

How can this "shared Canadian culture" be achieved? Clearly by making "unity in diversity" a living reality rather than trite cliché. While Canada has acted as an international leader by allowing many different ethnic communities, linguistic groups and geographical regions to retain their traditions, autonomy and identity, it has yet to create the commonalties of experience which are necessary to bind the various peoples of Canada together as a group. Without these commonalties of experience, there is the perpetual danger that greater emphasis will be placed on cultural differences rather than similarities, thereby exacerbating the various ethnic divisions, linguistic tensions, regional frictions and social disparities which exist throughout the country. True cultural integration will only be achieved when there are many more opportunities for cross-cultural understanding, dialogue, exchange, co-operation and fertilization among all the peoples, communities, provinces and regions of Canada.

CANADA'S INTERNATIONAL CULTURAL RELATIONS

While indigenous Canadian cultural development is achieved most effectively by developments on the domestic front and building up a culture which grows naturally and organically out of the roots, soil and traditions of the Canadian situation, it is manifested most readily by developments on the international front. For although it may be difficult for Canadians to differentiate between the imitative, imposed and indigenous patterns of cultural development in Canada, this is immediately apparent to people living outside the country. People in other parts of the world are instantly aware of whether Canada and Canadians are engaged in the indigenous, imitative or imposed pattern of cultural development, as this shows up most markedly in Canada's relations with other countries and the rest of the world.

Viewed from the holistic perspective advocated here, *all* relations involving Canada and other countries are cultural relations. Economic, political, diplomatic, commercial and technological relations are cultural relations in this sense every bit as much as artistic, scientific, academic and athletic relations. The reason for this is clear. Since all relations which Canada conducts with other countries make cultural statements of one sort or another, they are cultural relations in the best and fullest sense of the term.

Since the arts, sciences, humanities, and scholarship communicate the vitality, creativity and essence of Canadian culture better than anything else, they should be awarded top priority in Canada's system of international relations. This is in marked contrast to the present system. In the present system, economic, commercial and political relations are assigned top priority. The problem with this is that relations in these areas are cold and impersonal, largely because they are concerned with products rather than people. As a result, the human element is missing. But this is precisely why relations in the arts, humanities, sciences and scholarship are so essential. Human communication is their very essence. Thus a comprehensive programme of exchanges with other countries involving artists, scientists and scholars is exceedingly valuable because it communicates effectively across international frontiers and exposes people in other parts of the world to what Canada and Canadians are all about.

Using artistic, humanistic and scientific relations as the foundation or base, it does not prove difficult to visualize how a comprehensive and dynamic system of international cultural relations can be developed involving massive economic, commercial, diplomatic and political relations with the rest of the world. To be effective, such a system should be predicated on cultivating strong and dynamic relations with *all countries* and *all parts of the world.* On the one hand, this means strengthening Canada's relations with its traditional partners — France, Great Britain, the Commonwealth countries, la Francophonie, the United States and the like. On the other hand, it means striking out in new directions and forging strong and sustaining links with countries in Eastern and Western Europe, Africa, Asia, Latin America and the Caribbean. This so-called "third option," where Canada constantly and consistently acts to neutralize the danger of too much dependency on a few countries and especially the United States by developing a series of deep and dynamic relations with other countries and parts of the world, is no longer just another option. It is the only option if Canada wants to maintain its sovereignty and independence in the future. Mahatma Gandhi had wise advice in this regard: "I do not want my house to be walled in on all sides and my windows to be stuffed. I want the cultures of all lands to be blown about my house as freely as possible, but I refuse to be blown off my feet by any one of them."

THE ADMINISTRATION OF CANADA'S CULTURAL SYSTEM

It is impossible for Canada's governments to play a strong role in the evolution of Canada's network of international cultural relations and be fully involved in the country's domestic cultural development without becoming deeply immersed in the cultural life and affairs of the country. Is it possible for the country's governments to do this without stifling creativity, restricting the free flow of information and activities, hardening cultural patterns and arteries and producing in the end a culture which is pedantic, lethargic, introspective and nationalistic?

It is impossible to answer this question without plunging deeply into a consideration of the administration of Canada's cultural system. For, on the one hand, it is imperative for Canada's federal, provincial, municipal and territorial governments to ensure the development of a strong, vigorous, dynamic and sovereign Canadian culture — a culture capable of meeting the needs of Canadians for security, survival, health, material comfort and creative fulfilment. On the other hand, it is imperative for the country's governments to achieve this with a maximum amount of leadership and a minimum amount of interference.

While all governments in Canada have a fundamental role to play in the development of a strong, vigorous, dynamic and sovereign Canadian culture, the federal government has a particularly crucial role to play. Not only does the federal government occupy a position of fundamental importance in the development of Canadian culture in the fullest and most complete sense of the term — a position which cannot be assumed or played by any other level of government or the private sector — but also all other levels of government and the private sector take their lead from the federal government. Without strong leadership by the federal government, this most paramount need of all will not be met.

By providing strong leadership, the federal government will send out a clear signal to the other levels of government and the private sector that it is serious about Canadian culture and is deeply committed to developing the aims, objectives and programmes necessary to govern

Canadian cultural development and guide the administration of Canada's cultural system in the future.

What are these aims, objectives and programmes? Surely among the most essential are: assurance that the country possesses the cultural resources, options and opportunities which are necessary to satisfy citizens' needs; maximization of citizen participation in cultural life; creation of a shared Canadian culture which possesses a sufficient measure of unity, identity and diversity; and creation of a culture which is sovereign over its own affairs and in full control of its own destiny. While these are not the only aims, objectives and programmes which should govern Canadian culture and guide the administration of Canada's cultural system in the present and the future, adherence to them should go a long way towards ensuring that Canadian cultural development is dynamic, vigorous, vital and properly positioned in the natural and historical environment.

In the act of realizing these aims, objectives and programmes, it will be necessary for Canada's federal, provincial and municipal governments to establish the proper administrative structure and institutional infrastructure. Consistent with the administrative structure and institutional infrastructure which has already evolved in this area throughout the country, this administrative structure and institutional infrastructure should include both departments or ministries of cultural development as well as cultural agencies situated at arm's length from government and the political process. Not only has Canada been an international pioneer in the development of this type of administrative structure and institutional infrastructure[8] — largely through assimilation and adoption of the best features of the French and the British approaches to arts and cultural development — but also it is an administrative structure and institutional infrastructure which provides political clout within government through departments or ministries of cultural

---

[8] D. Paul Schafer. *Canada's Contribution to the International Practice of Arts Management.* Centre for Cultural Management. University of Waterloo. Waterloo. 1992. pp 38-39.

development as well as freedom from political interference and constraint through highly autonomous cultural agencies.[9]

As visualized here, departments or ministries of cultural development would be the most important departments or ministries in government — responsible directly to cabinets, parliaments and the political process. They would not be concerned with specific sectors of cultural activity as such, but rather with Canadian culture *as a whole*. Their principal function would be to link all government departments, ministries and agencies together in the common search for worldviews, values, value systems, programmes, policies and practices which are capable of guiding Canadian development most effectively in the future. Can there be any more important role in government and the political process than this?

Is there a clue here that is helpful in addressing the needs and concerns of Canadian culture in the future? Surely there is. It is impossible to deal with problems as difficult and demanding as cultural development, identity, sovereignty and survival without a total political commitment to culture — the kind of commitment which produces forceful departments or ministries in government charged with responsibility for culture in general and cultural development in particular. Such departments or ministries must have the authority, as well as the financial, administrative, capital and human resources, to formulate policies and activate developments in *all* fields of cultural endeavour.

History suggests that these responsibilities are best executed when they are carried out in accordance with the highest principles of creativity, excellence, access, freedom and participation. But as critics have repeatedly warned who have watched governments and departments or ministries of culture wrestle with the kinds of problems encountered in cultural development, permanent solutions to problems are not forthcoming without an equally strong commitment to freedom and independence — the kind of freedom and independence which comes from

---

[9] Harry Hillman Chartrand. *The Arm's Length Principle and the Arts: An International Perspective: Past, Present and Future.* Canada Council. Ottawa. 1985.

the creation of powerful and autonomous cultural agencies and a dynamic private sector capable of initiating programmes, allocating funds, animating activities and taking risks. Without both developments, co-operatively linked and systematically connected in an effective relationship, Canada will not be able to achieve the dynamic and distinctive cultural life successive generations of Canadians have been struggling to achieve.

A DYNAMIC CANADIAN CULTURAL POLICY

If Canadian culture is to thrive in the future, a comprehensive and coherent Canadian cultural policy is needed. Such a policy is required in order to translate the ideals, principles, aims and objectives of Canadian cultural development into workable procedures, priorities, strategies, tactics and practices.

Just as Canada's departments and ministries of cultural development should be linking mechanisms capable of uniting all government departments and agencies in the common quest to achieve a vital and viable culture, so Canadian cultural policy should perform a similar function. Its mission should be to link all policy fields together in the evolution of a balanced, diversified and enlightened attack on the development of Canadian culture as a whole.

Visualized in this way, cultural policy is a very different policy field than economic policy, social policy or political policy. Whereas these latter policy fields are concerned with specific parts of the whole, cultural policy is concerned with the whole itself. Its purpose is to ensure that the whole is structured and put together properly, and that there is a harmonious and synergistic relationship between the component parts of the whole.

This puts Canadian cultural policy on a very different plane from most if not all other policy fields. Whereas other policy fields are designed to develop the resources of specific sectors of Canadian culture

— industry, agriculture, trade, social affairs, recreation, the arts, communication, education and the like — Canadian cultural policy is designed to develop *all* these sectors in concert. It is the common thread, so to speak, that is needed to link all policy fields together and galvanize them into a unitary entity.

It follows from this that Canadian cultural policy must be accorded the highest priority in government and the political process as well as generally throughout Canadian society. Rather than being treated as a minor or insignificant branch of Canadian public policy, it should be treated as the heart and soul of Canadian public policy and dealt with accordingly. For just as Canada's cultural development is the principal raison d'être and responsibility of the country's governments, so Canadian cultural policy is the vehicle whereby this responsibility is translated into action. Perhaps this is why Gérard Pelletier, former Secretary of State and one of Canada's leading statesman, said Canadian cultural policy is "nothing more or less than a plan for civilization." It is a plan that requires utmost attention and involvement on the part of all governments and all citizens in the future.

THE FUTURE OF CANADIAN CULTURE

> Of all the middle powers, Canada has the greatest resources, the most central position, the finest web of contacts and influence and, relatively speaking, the highest proportion of experts both bilingual and in each language, of any nation in the world. If all these advantages were used not to affirm Canada as a state but develop Canada as a model-builder, then...the citizens who help recreate the world's image of itself might be recognized to have been citizens of Canada and Canada itself an "Athenian" variation on an Atlantic theme.
>
> Barbara Ward[1]

If Canadian culture is to thrive in the future, Canadians will have to make those fundamental changes in worldviews, values, value systems, lifestyles and living arrangements which are needed to develop a culture which is in tune with the newly-emerging global and Canadian reality. Having set the stage for an examination of these changes through a detailed assessment of the nature, scope, meaning and significance of Canadian culture in general and Canadian development in particular, the time has come to explore the changes which are needed if Canada is to maintain its dynamic, distinctive, creative and sovereign culture in the future.

THE NEW GLOBAL REALITY

There can be no doubt that a new global reality is taking hold and making its presence felt in the world. Not only is it bringing about fundamental changes in all aspects and dimensions of cultural life — economic, artistic, social, political, environmental, demographic, scientific, spiritual, and technological — but also it is touching every individual, institution, culture, country and continent.

---

[1] Barbara Ward. "The First International Nation." *The Canadian Forum.* October, 1968. Vol. 48. p. 153.

Clearly a new economic order is taking shape in the world. It is an order that suggests that the days of continuous growth and expansion are over and the days of consolidation, thrift, frugality and concern for survival are setting in. While some countries have been more fortunate than other countries in dealing with this situation, largely by being able to capitalize on pent-up consumer demand and carefully-devised monetary and fiscal policies, few countries have managed to escape reductions in disposable income and the material standard of living, declining levels of public and private subsidy, downsizing, privatization, increased unemployment and underemployment, higher taxes and mounting debts.

Added to these economic changes are all the political changes. Not only are the forces of liberalism, capitalism, conservatism, democracy and free trade blowing more and more freely throughout the world, but so also are the forces of nationalism, separatism, tribalism and isolationism.

These transformations in the economic and political landscape of the world are being matched by countless environmental changes. There is hardly a country, institution or individual anywhere in the world which is not fully aware of the state of the globe's fragile ecosystem, and with it, escalating levels of pollution and toxic substances, scarcities of renewable and non-renewable resources, holes in the ozone layer, and especially the need to achieve sustainable development and take the needs of future generations and the natural environment into account. Coupled with this are all the demographic and social changes which are taking place — the increasingly multicultural and multiracial character of society, the rapidly-expanding world population, changing relationships between men and women, growing concern for gender equality and social security, and the challenge of ageing and longevity.

It would be a mistake to underestimate the powerful effect that developments in technology and communications are having on all this. Not only is the computer revolution transforming economic, educational, industrial and commercial practices and relationships everywhere in the world, but explosive changes in this area are bringing to fruition

McLuhan's prophecy about "the global village." Not only are people being brought into closer and closer contact as borders collapse and communication technologies increase, but also there is a phenomenal increase in the collection, storage, retrieval and dissemination of information and electronic networking.

There is one final development which should be addressed since it appears destined to have a profound effect on people's lives and cultural development everywhere in the world. It is public and private reaction to globalization, the emergence of larger and larger trading blocks and free trade zones, the operations of multinational corporations, the creation of economic and commercial superstates and increased concentration of financial, industrial, marketing and technological power in fewer and fewer hands.

There can be no doubt that developments in this area are having a profound and unsettling effect on people everywhere in the world. As indicated earlier, this is manifesting itself in a number of countervailing movements aimed at giving people a greater say over the decision-making processes affecting their lives. Whether it is the quest for decentralization, sovereignty, identity and autonomy, or the resurfacing of interest in neighbourhoods and communities, the implications are everywhere much the same. Towns, cities, municipalities and communities are destined to play a much more important role in cultural development in the future than they have in the past.

It is against this backdrop that Canada and Canadians must etch their presence of the world of the future. It is a presence based on two fundamental considerations: all cultures are rapidly becoming "world cultures" in the sense that they are products of the global village and the revolution that is taking place in contemporary communications;[2] and Canadian culture has a seminal role to play in the world of the future by virtue of its unique characteristics and distinctive accomplishments.

---

[2] D. Paul Schafer. "Cultural Economies: Irresistible Forces Encounter Immovable Objects." *Futures: The Journal of Forecasting, Planning and Policy.* Vol. 26, No. 8, October 1994. pp. 830-845.

THE NEW CANADIAN REALITY

The fact that Canada is rapidly becoming a "world culture" like all other cultures in the world has important implications for the country and its citizenry. It means that Canadian culture — like Canada itself — must enter a new stage in its development — a stage which requires a number of fundamental changes in its overall design and basic composition.

What are some of these changes? Among the most important are: a greatly-expanded role for the country and its citizenry in international affairs; a vastly-altered role for the federal government in the cultural life of the country; a major redistribution of federal-provincial-municipal powers and responsibilities; cultivation of a more balanced set of cultural values and priorities; and last but far from least, creation of a more sensitive and compelling worldview. Reflection on each of these changes is rewarding since it provides the key to unlocking the secrets of Canada's development in the future.

If Canada is to play a forceful role in the world in the future, it will have to play a much larger role in international affairs.

While it is too seldom recognized at home, there is no doubt that Canada has an enormous credibility in the world as a result of its ability to confront and come to grips with a whole host of difficult and demanding economic, social, demographic and human problems. This has produced a number of assets and attributes which are recognized and respected internationally, such as the capacity for cultural creativity and innovation, the ability to produce high-quality artistic and industrial products, development of a progressive and dynamic educational and communications system, the capacity for compromise, concession, compassion and peace-keeping, and respect for the rights, equality, diversity and traditions of others. It is by no means coincidental that Canada has been selected by the United Nations as one of the most preferred countries in which to live. It results from a long tradition of solid and significant achievements, as well as a willingness to tackle complex problems and challenges.

These internationally-recognized facts place Canada in an ideal position to play a seminal and strategic role in world affairs in the future. It is an opportunity that is too important to be missed.

In order to do this, it will be necessary to greatly expand Canada's capacity for international relations and foreign affairs. Unfortunately, Canada's system of international relations and foreign affairs is under-developed and under-nourished at the present time, largely because it has been too dominated by other countries and restricted to a few regions or parts of the world. Historically, Canada's international relations and foreign affairs were confined to and dominated by Great Britain, France, Europe and the Commonwealth. Since the end of World War II, they have focused increasingly on the development of markets, trade associations and relations with the United States. Only recently have attempts been made to diversify Canada's international relations by cultivating relations with a number of Asian and Pacific rim countries. The consequences of these developments are all too apparent. Apart from the danger this represents in terms of Canadian cultural sovereignty, it has produced an international system for Canada and foreign policy posture which is too dependent on particular parts of the world. The solution to the problem is obvious. Much greater attention should be focused on developing dynamic and deepening relations with *all the countries and cultures of the world.*[3] Canada will only become a major player on the world scene and a leader in international affairs when it is doing much more cultural business with all the countries and cultures of the world.

A greatly-expanded system of international relations and foreign policy could enhance Canada's reputation for cultural diplomacy while simultaneously increasing its capacity for aid, trade, peace-keeping, peace-making, model-building and the like. Furthermore, it could provide the solution to the country's economic difficulties and inability to break out of a straightjacket characterized by tardy rates of economic growth, large public debts and high levels of unemployment.

---

[3] D. Paul Schafer. *Canada's International Cultural Relations.* Department of External Affairs. Ottawa. 1979.

A number of Canada's historical and contemporary assets and abilities should be pressed to the forefront here. One is the country's ability to produce high-quality products, from agriculture and industry to science, education and the arts. Another is the capacity to produce innovative technologies, particularly communications technologies which are in keeping with the rapidly-changing nature of global society. A third, and perhaps the most important of all, is Canada's increasingly multicultural and multiracial character. It does not take a great leap in imagination to recognize what an indispensable asset and valuable resource this is to the country and its citizenry. As a microcosm of the global macrocosm, Canada and Canadians possess the linguistic skills, entrepreneurial abilities and geographical contacts which are necessary to engage in innovative cultural undertakings in all parts of the world. All that is required now is the political will and public determination to take advantage of this vast reservoir of talent and ingenuity and develop it to the full.

Much of the leadership which is required for this should come from the federal government. Up to now, the federal government's role has been largely internal and domestic. In the future, it should be much more external and international. The federal government should set its sights squarely on making Canada a world leader on the international scene — not in the partial sense as a peace-keeper, aid-giver, conscientious-observer or compassionate ally — but rather in the total sense as an active and progressive participant in *all* aspects and dimensions of international affairs. Anything short of this will result in a serious short-changing of Canada's full potential and ability to play a meaningful and forceful role in the world of the future:

> ... a federal government, if it is to be successful, must accept the fact that its new, prime role is to work with other nations to manage global change for the benefit of humanity. Global policies mean that Ottawa must spend more time looking outward, rather than inward. It must recognize that to make Canada a better place, it must help to make the world a better place.[4]

---

[4] Tom Ford. "Role for Federal Government Awaits on Global Stage." *Toronto Star*. Tuesday, April 25, 1995. p. A15.

Redirecting federal efforts along international rather than domestic lines could help to solve two additional problems of critical importance to Canada and Canadians. The first has to do with the need to maintain a strong federal government. The second has to do with the need to redistribute governmental powers and responsibilities more judiciously.

During the last few decades, Canada's federal and provincial governments have been involved in a zero sum game. More power and responsibility to the provincial governments has been seen as a loss of power and authority for the federal government and its ability to play a strong central role. Hence the constitutional talks have always hinged on a seemingly unsolvable question: how can Canada maintain a strong federal government — which most agree is imperative for the long-term survival and continuity of the country — while simultaneously giving more power and responsibility to the provinces and particularly Quebec? It is clear where the answer to this question lies. It lies in viewing the situation from a dynamic and holistic rather than a static and specialized perspective. For in dynamic and holistic terms, there is ample opportunity to maintain a strong central government and simultaneously turn over more powers and responsibilities to the provinces. It is achieved by greatly expanding the federal government's role in international affairs. Such a development is not only in keeping with the role the federal government should be playing in an increasingly global and interdependent world, it is also in keeping with the principle of subsidiarity or assigning to each level of government the powers and responsibilities it is best equipped to handle.

A forceful development in this area could provide the key to renewed federalism and resolution of the constitutional problems with Quebec and the other provinces and territories of Canada. With the federal government playing a much stronger and more significant international role, it would be possible to re-negotiate federal-provincial powers in such a way that Quebec was given much more authority and control over such matters as training, immigration and the like which are imperative for preserving Quebec's distinct culture as well as its role as an indispensable contributor to Canadian cultural life. And by extending these powers and responsibilities to other provinces and the territories as well, it would be possible to maintain Canada's internationally-recognized reputation for dealing with all regions, provinces and territories equally and equitably.

In much the same way that making Canada an international leader could lead to a dramatic redistribution of federal-provincial powers and responsibilities, so it could lead to a dramatic redistribution of provincial-municipal powers and responsibilities. As indicated earlier, municipalities in Canada must be placed on a much stronger and more secure footing if they are to deal with the consequences of globalization and the need for much more solidarity, identity and control over decision-making. Without an equivalent redistribution of powers and responsibilities from the provinces to the municipalities — powers and responsibilities ranging all the way from jurisdictional arrangements to taxation and fiscal measures — it is difficult to see how Canada's municipalities will be able to deal with the demands and dictates of living in a dynamic and rapidly-changing world.

If fundamental changes are required in Canada's federal, provincial and municipal relations if Canada is to stay together and realize its full potential, fundamental changes are also required in Canada's cultural values and priorities.

Sustainable development will only be achieved in Canada when cultural values and priorities are established which are far less demanding on the natural environment and far more sensitive to the needs of people, other species, future generations and nature as a whole. Such values and priorities require a great deal of caring, sharing, co-operation, compassion, and emphasis on activities like the arts, education, ethics, social interaction and spiritual renewal which represent vastly different draws on the resources of nature. Thanks to the efforts of countless generations of Canadians and the country's historical and contemporary artists and scholars, many of these values and priorities are already deeply ingrained in the Canadian psyche. Pressing them to the forefront of Canadian development and consciousness at this time could prove exceedingly valuable and timely as the country prepares to confront the complex challenges and limitless opportunities of a new millennium.

Placing much more emphasis on qualitative as opposed to quantitative values and priorities could go a long way towards making it possible for Canadians to evolve a more sensitive and compelling worldview — a worldview which flows from a different set of axioms, assumptions, principles, perceptions and priorities. The basic features and fundamental characteristics of this worldview have been identified throughout the text: acceptance of the continuous line of Canadian cultural development dating back over thousands of years; recognition of the Indians and Inuit as the founding peoples of Canadian culture; acknowledgement of the rich contribution that all the diverse peoples of Canada have made and continue to make to Canadian cultural progress; affirmation of the principles of unity, equality, diversity, caring, sharing and co-operation; creation of a shared Canadian culture and indigenous pattern of Canadian cultural development; and willingness to respond to the call for international leadership.

Realization of this new worldview could go a long way towards establishing Canada's reputation as a "culture-maker" rather than a "culture-taker" in the eyes of other nations and the world as a whole. In order to perform this role, Canada will not only have to be in full control of its domestic and international affairs, it will also have to set the kind of example that other countries, cultures and peoples are anxious to follow. Execution of this role will require the capacity to give as well as to take, particularly as it relates to the country's natural resources, its unusual capacity for creativity and innovation, and its highly-developed technological acumen. For only in this way will Canada be able to make its full contribution to global progress and play a seminal role in ushering in a more human and humane world. Ultimately this is what Canadian culture and Canadian development are all about.

DESCRIPTION OF THE WORLD CULTURE PROJECT

The World Culture Project is a long-term research undertaking designed to promote the fact that culture has a crucial role to play in global development and world affairs in the future. It is being undertaken to coincide with and commemorate the World Decade for Cultural Development (1988-1997). For purposes of the Project, culture is defined in the holistic sense as worldview and values in general and a dynamic and organic whole in particular.

The Project has been subdivided into two components: an International Component and a Canadian Component. The International Component is designed to develop the holistic concept of culture in broad, general terms, as well as to apply it to a series of complex and persistent global problems. The Canadian Component is designed to develop the holistic concept of culture in specific, practical terms, as well as to apply it to a similar set of Canadian problems. As a case study, the Canadian Component offers a unique opportunity to examine the theoretical and practical implications of the holistic concept of culture for a country which may be called upon to play a seminal role in the new millennium.

Consistent with the division of the Project into two basic components, two monographs are developed each year, one for the International Component and one for the Canadian Component. A great deal of background research is undertaken in conjunction with each monograph and reactions are sought from advisory council members and authorities in the field. The topics of the monographs are:

INTERNATIONAL COMPONENT

The Character of Culture (1988)
The Politics of Culture (1989)
The Cultural Personality (1990)
The Community Culturescape (1991)
The Challenge of Cultural Development (1992)
Cultural Sovereignty and Change (1993)
International Cultural Relations (1994)
Cultural Education (1995)
Cultural History (1996)
Cultural Visions of the Future (1997)

CANADIAN COMPONENT

The Character of Canadian Culture (1988)
The Politics of Canadian Culture (1989)
The Canadian Personality (1990)
The Canadian Community Culturescape (1991)
The Challenge of Canadian Cultural Development (1992)
Canadian Cultural Sovereignty and Change (1993)
Canada's International Cultural Relations (1994)
Canadian Cultural Education (1995)
Canadian Cultural History (1996)
Visions of Canada's Cultural Future (1997)

For more information on the World Culture Project, please contact:

D. Paul Schafer
Director, World Culture Project
19 Sir Gawaine Place
Markham, Ontario
Canada, L3P 3A1
(905) 471-1342

ADVISORS TO THE CANADIAN COMPONENT OF THE WORLD CULTURE PROJECT

Greg Baeker	Toronto
André Fortier	Hull
Joy MacFadyen	Toronto
John Meisel	Kingston
Mavor Moore	Victoria
Walter Pitman	Toronto
Tom Symons	Peterborough
George Tillman	Ottawa
Steven Thorne	Vancouver
Paul Weinzweig	Victoria
Jiri Zuzanek	Waterloo